Perfect D

ALGARVE

Travel with
**Insider
Tips**

MARCO ⊕ POLO

Contents

 TOP 10   4

That Algarve Feeling   6

For chapters: See inside front cover

★ TOP 10

Not to be missed!
Our TOP 10 hits – from the absolute No. 1 to No. 10 –
help you plan your tour of the most important sights.

⭐1 PONTA DA PIEDADE ➤ 124

Enjoy picture-perfect views off the coast of Lagos – bizarre, majestic cliffs interrupted by a medley of natural arches and caves. They're best experienced on a boat tour.

⭐2 CABO DE SÃO VICENTE ➤ 127

Frequently whipped by hellish winds, this Cape, named after St. Vincent, plunges spectacularly down into the roaring sea below.

⭐3 PRAIA DA FALÉSIA ➤ 92

This magnificent beach is the sandy flagship of the Algarve. Overlooked by imposing walls of rust-red cliffs, the Praia's sweeping expanse of sand lies in the east of Albufeira, a popular holiday resort.

⭐4 OLHÃO ➤ 94

The fish market hall is a real high-light, and the fruit and vegetable stands are lively affairs, especially if you go on a Saturday.

⭐5 PRAIA DO AMADO ➤ 158

A wildly romantic, rugged Atlantic beach (image left, as seen at low tide) near Carrapateira. It's the perfect playground for surfers on the Costa Vicentina.

⭐6 IGREJA DE SÃO LOURENÇO ➤ 96

This small church on the edge of Almancil enchants visitors with its azulejos – the tiled décor here is extremely hard to beat.

⭐7 TAVIRA ➤ 66

With its river, churches, small castle, *camera obscura* and numerous refreshment stops, Tavira – the springboard for ex-ploring the Ilha de Tavira – boasts a selection of great attractions!

⭐8 RIO GUADIANA ➤ 70

This border river flows peacefully past Vila Real de Santo António, the castle town of Alcoutim, and the bird-rich wetlands of the Reserva Natural do Sapal.

⭐9 ILHA DA CULATRA ➤ 98

This island, home to the pretty villages of Culatra and Farol, is in a world of its own. The boat ride through the Ria da Formosa nature park is worth the trip alone.

⭐10 FARO ➤ 100

The Algarve's largest city surprises visitors with its harbour, its historic architecture and its vibrant, bustling atmosphere. Check out the well-preserved Old Town that's surrounded by mighty walls.

THAT
ALGARVE

Find out what makes the Algarve tick and experience its unique flair – just like the locals themselves.

LIFE'S A BEACH

Beaches might be a part of the *Algarvios*' lives from a young age, but that doesn't mean they let tourists hog all the best swimming and sunbathing spots for themselves! The Algarve's many beaches come in all shapes in sizes, ranging from the cliff-lined shores at the **Ponta da Piedade** (➤ 124) to the long expanses of sand near **Monte Gordo** (➤ 79) and on the **Ilha de**

Tavira (➤ 80). The region is a beach fan's dream come true!

FRESH FISH FROM THE GRILL

If you see columns of smoke in the air, it's nearly time to eat! These telltale signs come from simple restaurants and open-air grills that serve swordfish, salmon, sardines and a great deal more. It's a guaranteed taste sensation!

FUN IN THE SUN

Golf, standup paddleboarding, sea kayak tours… you'll find all this and more in the Algarve! The **Via Algarviana** (➤ 60) and the **Rota Vicentina** (➤ 42) are popular long-distance hiking trails, the **Costa Vicentina** (➤ 153) boasts some excellent surfing beaches, and the best cycling can be found along the 214km (133mi)-long **Ecovia** (➤ 179) that connects the **Cabo de São Vicente** (➤ 127) in the west with the **Rio Guadiana** (➤ 70) border river in the east.

The Algarve's magnificent beaches even look great on holiday snaps!

FEELING

There's something in the air above the Algarve: seagulls circle over colourful fishing boats off the coast of Lagos in the hope of nabbing some of the day's catch

That Algarve Feeling

MARKETS

No matter whether they're large or small, indoors or out, on the coast or inland… locals love their markets! They go there to stock up on fresh seafood, fruit, vegetables, honey, garlic, spices, sausages and cheese. The best markets in the region are held in **Olhão** (► 94) and **Loulé** (► 112). There's a bit of a carnival atmosphere there, particularly on Saturday mornings. Dive right in and enjoy the hustle and bustle!

STRAIGHT FROM THE SOURCE

Farmers and beekeepers go to markets to sell their wares – but locals also sell goods right outside their front doors! You'll often notice small crates or nets along the street filled with freshly plucked produce from the fields and private gardens. Depending on the season, you might stumble across

oranges, lemons, mandarines, melons and much more besides. Selling direct like this cuts out the middleman, and because there are no receipts, the taxman doesn't get a share either…

TAKING A BREAK

Taking a break is an essential part of life in the south, and no break would be complete without a spot of coffee! You could choose a tiny espresso *(café)*, which locals drink with plenty of sugar, or perhaps a large latte *(galão)* that's served in a glass – beware: holding this clear container without burning yourself demands a great deal of skill!

FROLICSOME FESTIVALS

The *Algarvios* might seem rather reserved, but they certainly know how to let their hair down during festivals. They celebrate Carnival for days on end in **Loulé** (► 112), the village of **Alte** (► 113) and elsewhere. Patron saint and summer festivals are also pretty lively. Get stuck in and party like a local!

BOTTLES OF LIQUID SUN

The region's wines (► 26), grown around **Alvor** (► 144), are a vital part of the Algarve experience. The reds are full bodied, the whites are smooth and fruity, and they all taste like they've been soaked in the southern sun!

The Algarve's orange harvest takes place in December and June

The Magazine

A MOORISH LEGACY

The Algarve meets North Africa

Our story starts in the 8th century, when the Moors followed in the footsteps of the Phoenicians, Greeks, Romans and Barbarians and conquered southern Portugal. Their culture and architecture influenced the region until the 13th century.

If you look and listen closely, you'll still see traces of the Moorish legacy all over the Algarve. The first clue is in the name of the region itself, which comes from the Arabic *Al Gharb* ("the West"). This refers to the western boundary of the Islamic Empire, a territory that stretched far across the Iberian Peninsula (the landmass that's home to Portugal and Spain today). The darker-skinned foreigners built towns, mosques, Quran schools and palaces in their new home, decorating them with horseshoe arches, wooden coffered ceilings, stone latticed windows and azulejos (➤ 30), the tiles that are still widespread today. The Moors' economic stalwarts included agriculture and textile production, and their trade routes spread out across the Mediterranean.

Whitewashed Houses and Well-stocked Pantries

The Moors liked to whitewash their houses. This is still a common sight in many villages today – in some parts of the Algarve, you might even feel as if you've been transported to North Africa. The Moors also placed a huge amount of significance on their pantries. Preserving food was a true

The Algarve's almond trees were introduced by the Moors

SIX SPOTS STEEPED IN MOORISH HISTORY

- **Silves** (➤ 140): The Castle of Silves and the Casa da Cultura Islâmica e Mediterrânica both testify to the Moorish presence in the area.
- **Mértola** (➤ 183): Head inside the Igreja Matriz in this small Alentejo town and you'll still see clear signs that the building was once a mosque. Even the horseshoe arches have been preserved.
- **Aljezur** (➤ 160): A whole room in the Museu Municipal is dedicated to the region's Islamic legacy.
- **Loulé** (➤ 112): Moorish ceramics number among the exhibits on display in the Museu Municipal de Arqueologia.
- **Lagos** (➤ 80): Check out the Moorish artefacts and archaeological findings in the Núcleo Islâmico. The collection includes ceramics.

art form that required the harmonious use of methods and materials in tandem. After all, making various foodstuffs stand the test of time was not simply a matter of drying them, salting them or immersing them in vinegar or honey – successful storage also required the right containers. Large, partially painted ceramic pots were used to store salted meat, pickled olives, olive oil, grain, water and a great deal more besides.

Cultural and Agricultural Advances

The Moors grew almonds, figs, citrus fruits and apricots, aided by the use of sophisticated irrigation techniques and encouraged by their particular fondness for gardens. Their economic progress and cultivation of highly evolved cultural and scientific advancements also meant that the Moors left their contemporaries in the western, Christian world entirely in the shade.

Away from the Algarve's coast, the Moors also transformed Silves into a thriving headquarters that is said to have even surpassed Lisbon – the capital of Portugal – in terms of its scale and importance in the

11th century. The poets, historians and lawyers of the age made Silves, then known as *Xelb* (or *Chelb*), their home. What's more, the poet Ibn Darraj Al Qastalli (958–1030) came from Cacela Velha – his memory lives on in the name of the square you'll spot as you stroll through the village today. Abû Al Abdarî, another 11th-century poet, also has a street named after him in Cacela Velha.

Little details like this street sign in Tavira provide hints of the Moorish legacy all over the Algarve

The almond blossom marks the start of spring – it often appears as early as January

Local sources herald the Castle of Silves as "Portugal's most beautiful military monument from the Islamic era". We should also add that it's been renovated extremely heavily – something you can't fail to miss if you take a walk through its grounds. The fortifications in Silves stand in stark contrast to other original Moorish castles like the one in Alvor, for instance, of which only tiny fragments have managed to survive the ravages of time.

Peace and Power Struggles

The Muslims and Christians sometimes coexisted in harmony. As proof of this, some people claim that a mosque and a monastery once stood side by side on the Cabo de São Vicente, long before anyone dreamt of building a lighthouse on the headland. It must be remembered that the Moors weren't a cohesive group, however, and were caught up in power struggles of their own over the years. The effects of these tussles reached all the way to the Algarve. After the mighty Caliphate of Córdoba – the nerve centre of Moorish power in Spain – collapsed in the 11th century, a number of small kingdoms were formed until two dynasties emerged: the Almoravids and the Almohads. The city of Tavira was conquered by the Almohads in 1167, but their presence there only lasted a few decades. Researchers have found evidence of a small Almohad quarter in the city. Located near the Convento da Graça – now a Pousada hotel – it consisted of a few houses around a central courtyard.

"Reconquest": From Minarets to Bell Towers

The *Reconquista* ("Reconquest") – the series of campaigns led by Christian forces to take back the Islamic territory in Europe – could not be fended off indefinitely. Their efforts relentlessly pushed down the border from the north. Spurred on by Royal backing and their distaste for Islam,

The Magazine

THE LEGEND OF THE SNOW

Although there are lots of slightly different versions of the tale, all *Algarvios* know the Legend of the Snow, a Moorish tradition handed down over the centuries. Once upon a time, a young, battle-hardened prince from Silves took a woman from northern Europe to be one of his wives. Said to be blond, blue-eyed and perhaps even a princess herself, the woman had been captured in battle, taken prisoner and carried far from home. Though the prince did nothing wrong, his new wife became gradually overwhelmed by a deep sadness. The reason was simple: she missed the snow of her homeland, which was nowhere to be seen in the sunny Algarve. Out of love for his bride, the prince had almond trees planted throughout his kingdom. At the start of every year, these trees began to bloom with their magnificent blossom and spread a carpet of white petals all over the land, making the countryside look as if it were covered in a fresh blanket of snow. This comforted the princess, and she and her husband have looked forward to the next year's almond blossom ever since.

The influence of the Moors can still be felt in the streets of Tavira

Archaeologists have excavated parts of a Moorish fortress at Silves Castle

the Orders of Knights also tossed their hats into the ring. The Christians overthrew, conquered and imposed their will on the Moorish people and their architecture. Mosques were converted into churches (sometimes just barely – see Mértola in the Alentejo region, for example) and minarets became bell towers (see the main church in Loulé). The Reconquista of the Algarve ended in the 13th century, far earlier than in neighbouring Andalusia, where the Nasrid dynasty managed to hold out until the fall of Granada in 1492. After the conquest, the Algarve was united with the Kingdom of Portugal.

Rediscovered by Archaeologists

At first glance, it looks as though time has wiped away many signs of the region's Moorish past. That's why archaeologists are still working hard to unveil the remaining traces of this bygone culture – check out their excavations of the Banhos Islâmicos (Islamic baths) behind a wall on the Largo de Dom Pedro I in Loulé's small Old Town, for example. Public baths played an important role in Islamic society, providing spaces to meet, chat and undergo cleansing rituals. Men and women used the baths separately. A hammam like the one in Loulé was divided into three zones: one hot, one warm, one cool. The bathing ritual started in the hot zone.

A Linguistic Legacy

During the many years of Moorish rule, a number of words were incorporated into Portuguese from Arabic that are still in use today. No fewer than 1,200 Portuguese words are of Arabic origin – one example is the term *aldeia*, meaning "village". Various place names in the Algarve also testify to the former Moorish presence in the region, including Algoz, Aljezur, Alvor, Alcantarilha, Almancil, Albufeira and Bensafrim. The name of the Rio Guadiana also comes from the Arabic *Wadi Yanah*.

PRINCE HENRY

A Sailor who Hardly Set Sail

Prince Henry, known as the Infante Dom Henrique in Portuguese, was a dominant figure in the late Middle Ages. The son of King João I and Philippa of Lancaster, he was influential in helping ignite Portugal's Age of Discovery. Born in Porto in 1394, he spent many years in the Algarve, living there until his death in 1460.

If you head to the Praça do Infante Dom Henrique in Lagos, you're guaranteed to come face to face with Prince Henry himself. You'll spot him sitting high up on a pedestal in the square, dressed in fine garments and looking at once majestic and serene. He appears illustrious and determined, and gives the impression of being a scholar. The monument's location was not chosen at random: in the gushing tones of one local source, Lagos is "the ideal stage from which to tell the tale of the great Portuguese Age of Discovery… for it was in this city – the largest in the Algarve at that time – that Prince Henry the Navigator planned the discovery of the African continent."

The Mythical Figurehead of the Portuguese Age of Discovery

Henry's nickname, "the Navigator" *(O Navegador* in Portuguese*)*, is misleading. Although he was involved in the Portuguese conquest of Ceuta in North Africa (1415), he wasn't aboard the *caravels* (Portuguese ships) when they set off on their famous Voyages of Discovery. Instead, he acted more as a planner and promoter behind the scenes. He also served as Governor of the Algarve and Grand Master of the wealthy Military Order of Christ.

Portuguese seafaring really got going under Henry and his father, João I. With the benefit of hindsight, it's tempting to view them as deliberately setting a plan in motion to discover pioneering maritime routes and eventually make Portugal a great colonial and trading power. All this was a long way off in Henry's time, however, and there is little chance that he could have imagined the consequences of his actions.

The Legendary Nautical School of Sagres

It has often been claimed that Henry decided to use the funds made available to him as Grand Master of the Military Order of Christ to set up a Nautical School in the Algarve. This place of learning reputedly gathered

Prince Henry depicted on a wall of azulejos in Sagres

Vela Lda

The Magazine

together a group of navigators, astronomers, shipwrights and cartographers in the Fortress of Sagres (➤ 129) to share their knowledge of seafaring. The original description of this academy comes from "*Hakluytus posthumus or Purchas: His Pilgrimes…*" a work published by the British travel writer Samuel Purchas (1577–1626) shortly before his death. The problem is that Purchas was writing generations after Henry's era, and never saw the institution himself. Although described in many books, it's rather unlikely that such a Nautical School ever existed.

COME FACE TO FACE WITH PRINCE HENRY

■ Fortress of Sagres (➤ 129)
■ Monument on the Praça do Infante Dom Henrique in Lagos (➤ 133)
■ Wax figure in the Museu de Cera dos Descobrimentos in Lagos (➤ 134)
■ Ermida de Nossa Senhora de Guadalupe (➤ 146), on the road between Lagos and Vila do Bispo. Prince Henry was said to have attended Mass frequently in this chapel.

It seems that all the accounts we have of the school were probably just dreamt up by people who quite fancied the image of Henry and his men working in a fortress high above the Atlantic, surrounded by spectacular scenery and views of the sea. Although various sources state that the Voyages of Discovery were very well planned, none of them say this took place in Sagres, or even necessarily under Prince Henry's leadership. In actual fact, the story of Portugal's blossoming maritime prowess is rather straightforward. After discovering the Azores in 1427, they simply chose to ignore the tales of terrifying sea monsters and magnetic mountains beyond and ventured further out along the west African coast, where Gil Eannes managed to round the legendary Cape Bojador in 1434.

The Dark Side of the Story

Financial interests naturally played a decisive role in the voyages of discovery. In order to increase his wealth and income, Henry had the foresight to sell trading licences to merchants that would allow him to secure some of the potential profits for himself. Over time, the African trade routes became more and more lucrative, in part due to the importation of slaves, terrifying numbers of whom were carried off to the Portuguese mainland. The first slave market took place in Lagos – the ships' main operational base – in 1444, well within Henry's lifetime. It was the start of a dark chapter in the Age of Discovery, the zenith of which – from a Portuguese point of view – came some decades after Henry's death in 1460. At its peak, the explorers celebrated triumph after triumph: Bartolomeu Dias rounded the Cape of Good Hope, Vasco da Gama charted a sea route to India, and Pedro Álvares Cabral arrived in Brazil in 1500. As these "triumphs" led to colonial rule in South America, the subjugation of whole cultures, unfathomable suffering and the importation of slaves in their millions, however, we might choose to view them in a different light today. And although Henry was long dead by then, he was nevertheless partly to blame.

Historians Drag the Hero from his Pedestal

For this reason alone, the heroic claims you'll often hear made about Henry are rather misplaced. This royal scion may well have been talented and educated, but was he really such a visionary or a scientific polymath as he is often portrayed? This remains to be seen. Portuguese historians, including António Henrique de Oliveira Marques (1933–2007), have sought to put the significance of Henry and his contributions into perspective. Oliveira Marques saw Prince Henry the Navigator as a life-long militarist and expansionist, to whom the conquests in the north of the African continent were much more important than any of his nation's more far-flung Voyages of Discovery. What's more, having an interest in astrology, astronomy, mathematics and nautical sciences was commonplace in the aristocratic circles of the era, and receiving foreigners and listening to their stories was by no means unusual. To cap it all, commercial interests and a love of profit were of the highest priority as far as Henry was concerned.

As the governor of the Algarve and Ceutas – two places where shipping and fishing were of great importance – the Prince quickly realised precisely how profitable the sea could be if only you knew how to exploit it properly. This was the argument put forward by Oliveira Marques, whose work, the "History of Portugal and the Portuguese Empire" gave examples of Henry's control in the Algarve: "In this way, [Henry] secured himself the monopoly on tuna fishing throughout the Kingdom of the Algarve, a tenth of the total catch made by the fishermen in Monte Gordo, and privileges and income from hunting young tuna and corvina."

Whatever you think about Prince Henry the Navigator, one thing becomes clear on closer inspection: the stories surrounding him are a mixture of history and mythical glorification, fuelled by authors from the 16th century. Such early writers as Giovanni Battista Ramusio and Damião de Góis attributed qualities to him that he likely never possessed. All in all, Henry's legendary image has to be taken with a big pinch of salt.

The fortress on the Cabo de São Vicente near Sagres looks defiantly out to the Atlantic – was this once the location of Henry's seafaring school?

ABSOLUTELY
CORKING!

Cork oaks. You'll spot these gnarled, majestic trees all over the Algarve. Every nine years, their cork is stripped away, leaving their trunks shining with a honey-coloured glow that gradually turns rust-red. Once harvested, the cork is dried and processed in a huge variety of ways – champagne and wine corks are just the tip of the iceberg...

In fact, it's hard to believe how many things you can make from wrinkled bits of bark! The tree it grows on is the cork oak *(Quercus suber)*, known as *sobreiros* in Portuguese. It's undemanding, evergreen and something of a national symbol. Despite competition from Spain and Morocco, Portugal is the world's biggest cork producer – you'll see it growing over hundreds of thousands of acres throughout the country.

Cork oaks are stripped every nine years and grow to form fairy-tale forests

The cork is piled high after being harvested from May to September

A Financial Powerhouse by the Side of the Road

The fascinating world of cork is just waiting to be discovered in the Algarve's hilly hinterland, a place where the air is wonderfully fresh and the birds chirrup away in the branches above. It's here you'll get to drive through the cork forests that play such a key role in the Algarve's economy. Cork oaks aren't just there for decoration, after all – they've long been connected with industrial production. Proof of this is found in the stacks of cork you'll

HOW TO GET ACQUAINTED WITH THE WORLD OF CORK

■ You'll find examples of cork oak forests in the **Serra de Monchique** (▶ 136), the **Serra do Caldeirão** (▶ 113) and around **São Brás de Alportel** (▶ 109).

■ Check out the **Museu do Traje** in São Brás de Alportel (▶ 109). A museum annex there is home to an extremely informative department dedicated to all things cork.

■ If you're interested in organised cork tours, get in touch with **Rota da Cortiça** (São Brás de Alportel, tel. 289 840 018, mobile/cell 960 070 806; info@rotadacortica.pt; www.rotadacortica.pt).

■ Cork tours are also offered by **Algarve Rotas** (Mesquita Baixa, São Brás de Alportel, mobile/cell 918 204 977; e-mail: turismo@algarverotas.com; www.algarverotas.com).

---

see piled up by the side of the road during the cork harvest season (between the end of May and September). These often elongated piles are primarily designed to attract the attention of potential buyers as they pass. The way the stacks are assembled allows professionals to get a quick estimate of the number of kilos they're looking at, and thus the price they should offer to the owners.

The Art of Stripping

Stripping the bark – a job that calls for a veteran cork harvester – requires just as much skill as stacking it afterwards. All of the work is done by hand, but doesn't need any muscle power at all. The workers rely on years of experience and their feel for the material to split the bark with an axe and remove as large a piece as possible. A single harvester can work dozens of cork oaks a day. The harvest, which takes place every nine years, is only carried out on the lower part of the trunk. Afterwards, a brush is used to mark the last digit of the year it was harvested. For example, a 6 means that it was stripped in 2016, and shouldn't be worked again until 2025. Cork production is a waiting game: a cork oak is only ready to be stripped when it's 25 to 30 years old. And even then, it will only start producing good quality cork after its first couple of harvests. On the plus side, the trees can easily reach a ripe old age of 150 to 200 years, meaning that they can be profitably stripped anywhere up to 16 or 17 times during their lives.

One Man's Hut is Another Man's Cork Factory...

Various cork factories can be found in and around the country town of São Brás de Alportel. They've been there for a very long time. In the second half of the 19th century, the cork industry began to spread in the surrounding regions. At some point, a few donkey drivers who had previously only transported the material got a taste for business and set about producing it themselves. As a result, they set up dozens of cork

Old, mighty cork oaks are a defining feature of much of the Algarve

From left to right: the cork harvest requires expertise and nimble fingers; unique cork shoulder bags, each with their own individual grain; the cork department at the costume museum in São Brás de Alportel

"factories" – a rather grandiose term for what were often little more than simple huts. These workshops were kitted out with a cauldron for boiling the cork (to get rid of insects and make it more flexible), a workbench for cutting the material and a press for bundling it up. Back then, corks used in bottles had to be painstakingly manufactured by hand by carving small cubes to size and rounding them off. The profits made from the industry spawned a number of swanky villas and triggered the emergence of a prosperous middle class in São Brás de Alportel.

Processing: Nature has the Last Word

Cork production still takes the same basic form today. The harvested raw material is initially left in piles until the bark and all its resins are completely dried out – a process that can take several years. When it's ready, the bark is then boiled in the factory. What happens next (pressing, further drying and cutting) is an extremely complex process. Since it's a natural material, there may be thinner and thicker areas in the same piece of cork bark. And when you cut through it, you might discover that it's been damaged by vermin. Cork with such defects isn't good enough to be made into high-quality stoppers for wine, prosecco or champagne bottles – low grade cork bark is used to make granules for other products instead.

From Stopping Bottles to Stopping Draughts

Cork has many qualities and advantages that people have appreciated and employed since time immemorial. For example, workers used to take cooked food with them into the fields in cork containers to help keep it warmer for longer. They also found that spoons made from cork were excellent for scooping up water, soups and stews. Cork is light, easily pressable, slightly flexible and recyclable. It also deadens noise and

repels water, making it ideal for thermal and acoustic insulation. Today, cork is employed in an almost unbelievable number of tasks. The classic product is still, of course, the good old bottle cork – slim ones for wines and larger ones for bubbly. Beyond this, however, cork is used to insulate houses in Scandinavia and North America, produce handles for Nordic walking sticks, and make flooring, coasters and orthopaedic insoles. As if that weren't enough, cork is also found in baseballs, golf balls and shuttlecocks for badminton.

The Latest Fashion: Cork Leather

In recent times, cork has also become popular in the design and fashion worlds. After a lengthy conversion process, cork can be used to create "cork leather", an alternative to using animal skins. "If you love leather but don't want to hurt any animals, try cork leather for size" – so say the leaders of the Rota da Cortiça cork route initiative that's been established in São Brás de Alportel (▶ 23, box).

> "If you love leather but don't want to hurt any animals, try cork leather for size!"

Thanks to a dash of artisanal creativity, cork leather has been used to make a wide range of original fashion pieces: handbags and purses, belts, shoes, iPad cases, ties, caps, hats, mouse mats and a great deal more besides.

If you get a chance, try running your hand over the material: it feels soft and downright velvety. Cork leather is also used to give a stylish twist to all kinds of jewellery, including bracelets, necklaces, rings, earrings and pendants. You can even buy umbrellas and wedding dresses made of the stuff. One thing's for sure, the natural, highly distinctive flow of the grain makes each piece of cork leather absolutely unique – it's the perfect way to express your individual style!

WINES of the ALGARVE
Bottled Sunshine

The Phoenicians, Greeks and Romans were all involved in the Portuguese wine trade. *Vinho* was also an important export during the Middle Ages. Whether you're looking for reds, whites or rosés, the varieties from the Algarve now have a permanent place in Portugal's wine scene.

The wines here smell so good – they're woody, richly fruity and thrilling! As soon as you step into an Algarve winery, you'll catch the heady scent of the tasty treats in store. The region is great for growing grapes thanks to its ideal climate (dry and hot with relatively low temperature changes and over 3,000 hours of sunshine a year), its diverse soils and its proximity to the Atlantic. What's more, the area's winegrowers benefit from the warm winds that blow up from North Africa and the nearby mountains and hills that shield their vines against cooler breezes from the north. All of this results in the Algarve's distinctive wines that taste like sunshine in a bottle.

Grape Varieties, Growing Regions and the Wine Revival

The Algarve's traditional grape varieties are *Negra Mole* and *Castelão* for red wines and *Síria* and *Arinto* for whites. Once seen across the region, winegrowing almost completely disappeared from the Algarve, due not in small part to being ousted by the development of large-scale hotel and

---

VISITING A VINTNER

Make enquiries in advance if you want to visit the big warehouse of the Adega Cooperativa do Algarve wine cooperative. A tour of a winery (including wine tasting) costs around €7.50–€10 per person.

- **Quinta dos Vales:** Sítio dos Vales, Estômbar, tel. 282 431 036; quintados vales.eu; Mon–Fri 9–noon, 2–6pm; accommodation and an art collection.
- **Adega Quinta do Morgado da Torre Sítio da Penina:** Alvor (take the signposted turn-off from the N125 near Alvor), tel. 282 476 866; www.morgadodatorre. com, Mon–Fri 10–noon and 2–5pm.
- **Adega do Cantor – Quinta do Miradouro:** Guia, tel. 289 572 666; www. winesvidanova.com, Mon–Fri 10am–1pm and 2–5pm.
- **Adega Cooperativa do Algarve:** Estrada Nacional 125, Lagoa, tel. 282 342 181; adega.lagoa@sapo.pt, Tue–Sat 10am–1pm and 2–6pm; the cooperative's building is also home to the Arte Algarve art initiative.

The Magazine

housing complexes. Despite this, the region's wines have been making a strong comeback since around the turn of the millennium. You'll now see vineyards near the coast by Alvor as well as further inland towards Querença. What's more, Lagoa is home to the **Adega Cooperativa do Algarve** wine growers' association, and none other than the famous British pop singer Sir Cliff Richard has successfully invested in a winery himself – the **Adega do Cantor** near Guia. New grape varieties have also been introduced in many areas. The four growing regions with a coveted 'protected designation of origin' – the *Denominação de Origem* – are Lagoa, Lagos, Portimão and Tavira. Organic wines *(vinhos biológicos)* are becoming more and more prevalent.

Quality Wines and Experimental Vintners

Armed with modern viticultural principles and some very exacting standards, a number of forward-thinking winemakers sought out the best locations in the region and started focussing on quality rather than quantity – you won't find any signs of mass production in the Algarve. A prime proponent of the renaissance in top-class local wines is the **Quinta dos Vales** by Estômbar. Its oldest vineyards date from the late 1990s, and they employ such cutting-

---

TASTING NOTES

Whatever you do, don't miss the chance to go wine tasting. The following tasting notes will give you some idea of what to expect:

- **White wines:** light and dry yet fruity; citrus colours; aromas include green apples, pears, peaches, tropical fruits (pineapples, passion fruits, bananas and tangerines, for example), and sometimes even a slight hint of asparagus.
- **Rosés:** balanced, dry, fresh and fruity; strong aromas of red fruits (strawberries and raspberries) along with some notes of blackberries and such tropical fruits as guava.
- **Red wines:** strong colour compositions ranging from ruby red to black cherry; aromas include dark plums, red and black berries, spices, white pepper and chocolate.

edge technology as temperature-controlled fermentation and stainless steel tanks. But never fear: they still use oak barrels, an essential part of the winemaking process. They're also constantly carrying out experiments on their 19ha (47 acres) of predominantly chalky land – they've tried planting new grape varieties, for instance, including *Syrah, Cabernet Sauvignon, Touriga Franca, Touriga Nacional* and *Alicante Bouschet.*

Grape vines beginning to grow in the spring (above); the cellar at the Adega do Cantor, Cliff Richard's vineyard (left)

Award-winning Wineries: Large Companies and Family-run Businesses

The vines at the **Quinta dos Vales** are pruned between late December and mid-February. The grapes themselves are harvested by hand from the start of August to September. In some places, you'll even see harvesters at work well into October. The growers at Quinta dos Vales are fond of telling people that "all of [their] vineyards are watered by a drip irrigation system." They've won numerous prizes for their wines, but then so have such family-run wineries as the **Adega Quinta do Morgado da Torre**, which use much more modest technology. Tasting and buying wines direct from these vineyards all over the Algarve is a real pleasure.

AZULEJOS

Azulejos are the ceramic tiles that form such a typical part of Portugal's style. They adorn entire house facades and courtyards, church walls and benches, and are also used to make door and window frames. If you're holidaying the Algarve, you'll spot azulejos everywhere you go.

Locals are used to seeing them from an early age, but visitors never cease to marvel at the wealth of azulejos murals and colour compositions on show in the region. If you keep your eyes peeled as you travel through the Algarve, you'll be delighted by the sheer diversity of the tiles and the way they shine in blue, white, yellow and many other nuanced tones. You'll see them wherever you go – in Faro, Tavira, Vila Real de Santo António, Alvor and even in the tiny parish of Alferce in the Serra de Monchique. It's no exaggeration to say that the Algarve's towns and villages look like open-air azulejos museums. Tiles also line the interiors of many buildings and churches – for a prime example, take a peek inside the Igreja de São Lourenço dos Matos on the outskirts of Almancil.

Décor with a Rich History

The Moors were the original creators of azulejos – they referred to them as *al zuleique*, meaning "small, smooth, polished stones". After the Muslims were driven from power in the Iberian Peninsula, their tasteful, decorative wall and floor tiles didn't merely remain behind, but began to experience a steady growth in popularity. Before the Portuguese began to make azulejos for themselves, King Manuel I – the namesake of the magnificent Manueline architectural style – had them ordered in bulk from the Spanish city of Seville. Later rulers and clerics also developed a taste for the tiles. This was not lost on people lower down the social scale – after all, what was good enough for the royals and God's representatives on earth was good enough for them! People soon began to decorate their house facades, staircases, gardens, fountains and terraces with azulejos. The Portuguese

Azulejos images often show biblical scenes (left) or such historical compositions as the coronation of Peter IV (below) and the granting of the Constitution in 1826

embraced the tiles more whole-heartedly than in any other European country. The south of Spain is the only other place where you'll see them used in a similar way.

Declarations of Faith and Practical Purposes

The sheer variety of tile motifs is enormous. Ceramic tiles are used to make billboards for businesses, cafés and restaurants. You'll also see

Originally of Moorish origin, azulejos tiles experienced their heyday in the Portuguese Baroque when they were often used to adorn church walls. They're also popular as decorations on the doorways and facades of houses, like this one in Tavira

them employed in street signs and municipal coats of arms. Geometric and floral patterns are popular, too, as are large designs that cover whole walls and depict saintly, traditional and historical scenes. The colours on the azulejos are never a motley mishmash of tones, but always harmonise beautifully with one another.

Although the colourful tiles are used for decoration, they're not just there for show. Some homeowners place small azulejos images of Christ or the Virgin Mary on their house facades to profess their faith and give their buildings a layer of symbolic protection. As far as they're concerned, it also doesn't hurt to put an image of Saint Barbara on your home to shield it from fires and storms. Covering entire facades in decorative azulejos also has a practical purpose that goes beyond mere embellishment. Azulejos are pleasantly cool, and any wall covered in the tiles is less vulnerable to moisture. What's more, these popular Portuguese ceramics also help to dampen any noise travelling in from the street.

Attentive visitors will spot azulejos tiles adorned with the city of Faro's historic coat of arms

Open-air Art and Souvenirs

Any journey through the Algarve is a trip through the world of the azulejos. It's a wonderful artistic experience that doesn't cost a penny and is guaranteed to fill the memory cards of keen photographers. Azulejos also make nice souvenirs – they're weather resistant, simple to install and easy to transport.

TOP THREE: CHURCHES WITH AZULEJOS

You'll frequently come across beautiful azulejos decorations in such churches as the Sé (cathedral) in Faro (➤ 100) and the Igreja de Santo António in Lagos (➤ 133). For a superlative experience, however, check out our list of the very best tiled churches and chapels in the Algarve:

Insider Tip

- The **Igreja de São Lourenço dos Matos** on the outskirts of Almancil (➤ 96)
- The **Ermida de Nossa Senhora da Conceição** in the historic centre of Loulé (➤ 113)
- The **Igreja da Misericórdia** in the historic district of Tavira (➤ 67)

Culinary
CREATIONS

Restaurants all over the Algarve will get your taste buds tingling with such melt-in-your-mouth delicacies as exquisitely soft fish and delicious portions of cockles. Despite the decline of the local fishing grounds, the sea still plays a decisive role in the region's cuisine.

Fish and shellfish are vital components of the Algarve's culinary landscape. Seafood fans will be in absolute heaven here, tasting the fresh catch of the day – grilled or from the oven – with a beautiful view of the sea. Simple restaurants often serve food of such quality that you would happily give them a full complement of stars for their excellent cuisine. The *cataplana*, a copper cooking pot with a closable lid, is a popular tool in Portuguese kitchens that's used to prepare wonderful creations involving fish, shellfish, meat and/or pieces of sausage with vegetables, onions and potatoes, etc. To top it all off, enjoy your meal with an Algarve wine (► 26).

From Sardines to Monkfish
Grilled sardines *(sardinhas assadas* or *sardinhas grehadas)* are a classic Algarve dish. You'll also often see mackerel *(carapau)* and dried salt-cod *(bacalhau)* – a food that's popular all over Portugal – making an appearance on the menu. Discerning fish fans enjoy eating shellfish *(pescada)*, gilt-head bream *(dourada)*, tuna *(atum)*, sea bass *(robalo)*, sole *(linguado)*, mullet *(salmonete)* and swordfish *(peixe espardarte)*. Grilled tuna and swordfish steaks are served with mayonnaise, butter and lemon – otherwise they can be a little dry. Monkfish *(tamboril)* is often marinated (in a mixture of lemon juice, olive oil, salt, parsley and pepper) before being served on a skewer along with a selection of onions, bacon and peppers. Monkfish rice *(arroz de tamboril)* is also a popular choice. The region's restaurants usually only serve it in portions for two or more people.

Cockles and Barnacles
The range of tasty crustaceans on offer include little cockles *(amêijoas)* cooked in olive oil, garlic, coriander and sometimes a slug of white wine. Sophisticated palates will also enjoy goose barnacles *(percebes)*. They're harvested from the rocks with extreme effort and some highly

FRESH FROM THE SEA

amêijoas – cockles
atum – tuna
carapau – mackerel
dourada – gilt-head bream
linguado – sole
lulas – squid
peixe espardarte – swordfish
percebes – goose barnacles
pescada – shellfish
polvo – octopus
robalo – sea bass
salmonete – mullet
sardinhas – sardines
tamboril – monkfish

dangerous manoeuvres by professional collectors, which explains their high price. Don't be put off by their appearance: goose barnacles are part of the crustacean family. They're far from beautiful, however, and don't look much like the classic molluscs you'll usually see on the menu.

Squid and Octopus
Some people see goose barnacles as a real delicacy, while others view them as a highly acquired taste. The same goes for small squid *(lulas)* and octopus *(polvo)*. Octopus with boiled potatoes *(polvo à lagareiro)* is a popular choice in the region. Squid is often cooked in a skillet before being quickly braised in some white wine. It's also

José Pinheiro from Vila do Bispo is regarded as the *Cataplana* King (above); this seafood *cataplana* (middle) is one of his specialties; goose barnacles (below) are one of the most popular seafood dishes in the Algarve

The Magazine

Hearty chouriço sausages are a speciality from the region around Tavira

sometimes served stuffed with a filling made from its own finely chopped tentacles and little pieces of vegetable (onion and carrot, for example).

For Carnivores

Visitors to the Algarve can try *carne de porco à alentejana*, a delicious pork dish with cockles that originates from the neighbouring region of Alentejo to the north. Grilled lamb chops *(costeletas de borrego grelhadas)* with mint sauce are also very popular. Steak *(bife)* is a reliable choice. Grilled chicken *(frango assado)* is a cheaper alternative that locals love to eat with spicy piri piri sauce.

One for the Road...

The typical post-dinner tipple of choice in the Algarve is *medronho*, a strong, clear brandy made from the fruit of the strawberry tree. It often contains around 50% alcohol and can pack a bit of a punch. Strawberry trees full of red fruits can be seen in such places as the Serra de Monchique, where the drink is also made.

A MEDITERRANEAN DIET BY THE ATLANTIC

The inhabitants of the Algarve – a region by the Atlantic – tend to eat like the Mediterraneans. They follow the *dieta mediterrânica*, a way of eating that helps prevent cardiovascular disease. The Ten Commandments of this famous "Mediterranean diet" are as follows:

1. Olive oil is the main source of fat for frying, cooking and dressings.
2. Eat plenty of fresh vegetables and fresh and dried fruits; it's also important to use garlic.
3. Whatever you do, don't miss out on bread and cereals.
4. Wherever possible, eat seasonal fruits that are as organic as possible.
5. Add dairy products like yogurt and cheese to your diet.
6. Only eat red meat and eggs in moderation.
7. Treat yourself to plenty of fish.
8. Only eat sweet treats on special occasions and make fruit your go-to dessert.
9. Drink water more than anything else, but a small glass of red wine with dinner is very much encouraged.
10. A little exercise every day is just as important as a balanced diet.

FLORA and FAUNA

The Algarve's natural surroundings will stimulate all your senses. The air is filled with the scent of herbs and the breeze blows through eucalyptus trees, mimosas and umbrella pines. It's so lush you can almost taste it. Storks nest on roofs and flamingos pace around on stilt-like legs. And no holiday would be complete without a spot of snorkelling.

The region's flora and fauna give the south of Portugal a magnificently exotic flair – something you'll start to sense soon after you arrive. Even veteran visitors to the Algarve never stop marvelling at the Mediterranean vegetation you stumble across in the region, including prickly pears, agaves, mimosas, junipers, lavender, sea pinks, dwarf fan palms and oleanders. And as far as the fauna is concerned, you'll spot the most spectacular species the animal kingdom has to offer if you go bird-watching or venture underwater.

Oranges and Almonds, Palm Trees and Rockrose Shrubs
Many *Algarvios* make a living from the region's orange and almond trees and earn their keep from the cork oaks you'll spot further away from the coast. Carob, olive and pomegranate trees also thrive in the Algarve alongside figs, lemons, mandarins and medlar. Evergreen oaks and strawberry trees covered in bright red fruits can also be found in the mountains. Although they smell fantastic, nature experts view eucalyptus trees as pests – they grow extremely quickly and leach far too many nutrients from the soil. Fig-marigolds are also tarred with the same brush.

The Magazine

Hibiscus bushes and palm trees are planted for decoration. Vast areas along the **Costa Vicentina** (➤ 153) are covered in naturally occurring rockrose shrubs that flower from March to May. Spring is the best time to see the Algarve's patchwork of plants in full bloom. The vegetation on the Costa Vicentina, which largely consists of macchia plants and bushes, is kept low and pressed to the ground by strong winds.

The Kingdom of the Flamingos

The Algarve is a true paradise for birdwatchers: several hundred species of bird have been documented in the region. It's especially fun to watch pink flamingos pick their way through the wetland landscape with inimitable elegance and comb the water with their sieve-like beaks for tiny brine shrimp, their favourite food. Flamingos aren't just temporary guests in the Algarve who pack up and leave for Africa when winter draws near – they're now increasingly staying all year round. Photographers love capturing them as they take off clumsily from the ground and rise up into the

Insider Tip

TOP SPOTS FOR BIRDWATCHERS

You'll have a great time if you remember to bring some binoculars and a camera with a powerful zoom or telephoto lens. Bird-watching is also a fantastic activity for 👪 families with kids – and it doesn't cost a penny! Top bird-watching spots include:

- The **Parque Natural da Ria Formosa** (➤ 108) near Faro and Olhão (➤ image below: flamingos in the salt fields around Olhão).
- The **Ria de Alvor** near Alvor (➤ 145).
- The salt marshes and the **Reserva Natural do Sapal** (➤ 78) near Castro Marim.
- The **Lagoa dos Salgados** (➤ 139), a lake near Armação de Pêra.
- The **Parque Natural do Sudoeste Alentejano e da Costa Vicentina** (➤ 155) on the Costa Vicentina.

If you go dolphin watching, you might just spot a whole family swimming by

air in formation. When they're flying, they look just like pink hair clips soaring through the sky!

Storks, Herons and Eagles

Strange as it seems, you'll see white storks' mighty nests – each of which can weigh more than 50kg (110lbs) – in such towns as Faro and Portimão. Being near people and noisy streets doesn't seem to bother them at all. Various species of gull can also be spotted in abundance along the coast. You'll need a little more luck and perseverance to spot great egrets, little egrets, kingfishers, western swamp hens, spoonbills and shags (a member of the cormorant family). You can also see curlews, redshanks, black-winged stilts, oystercatchers, pied avocets, Kentish plovers, curlew sandpipers and sandwich terns. If you're extremely fortunate, you might glimpse ospreys, peregrine falcons and Bonelli's eagles. The Atlantic's huge tidal range provides a great deal of food for them all. Lots of small creatures are left behind in the mud at low tide and are a perfect target for thousands of hungry beaks.

Dolphins and Seahorses

If you take a tour out to sea from somewhere like Lagos (➤ 135) you'll have a good chance of spotting dolphins of the bottlenose, striped, spotted and common varieties. Diving trips also give you the chance to come face to face with squid, European conger eels and starfish. If you're feeling exceptionally lucky and want to stay on dry land, head to the **Parque Natural do Sudoeste Alentejano e da Costa Vicentina** where you might just spot one of the foxes or Iberian lynx that have sometimes been sighted there. Otters and chameleons are a rarity in the **Parque Natural da Ria Formosa**, which is also home to two types of seahorse. Although they're shy and like to stay hidden away, there are some tour operators who'll kit you out with snorkels and carefully bring you as close as possible to these tiny critters. The seahorse colony in the Parque Natural da Ria Formosa is one of the largest in Europe.

HOLIDAYS in the COUNTRYSIDE

If you want to discover an entirely different side of the Algarve and have a peaceful, stress-free holiday, stay in a country house – it's a unique type of tourism that's incredibly relaxing indeed.

Birds twitter all around, soft winds rustle through the olive and orange trees, there's no engine noise to be heard, and beautiful, sweeping vistas draw your eyes to the hills nearby. *Turismo Rural* (rural tourism) is the best choice for anyone who really wants to chill out and have a completely different Algarve experience. It's a chance to unwind and take your holiday at your own, relaxed pace. Depending on the accommodation you choose (► see box below), the atmosphere will be down-to-earth or provide a touch of exclusivity with lots of amenities. You can rent a whole house or a room in a rural guesthouse.

A Real Refuge

Country house lodgings are real refuges – peaceful corners tucked away that offer nature fans a taste of largely unspoilt rural life. Staying in the countryside doesn't narrow your options down, either: if you have a car (something we highly recommend!) you can easily make it to the beaches and the coast for a day trip. Everywhere in the Algarve has everything you'll need for a great holiday. A good base in the eastern Algarve is the late-19th-century **Herdade da Corte** country estate that lies inland from

COUNTRY HOUSE ACCOMMODATION

- **Herdade da Corte**, Sítio da Corte, Santa Catarina da Fonte do Bispo, tel. 281 971 625; www.herdadedacorte.com
- **Quinta do Mel**, Olhos d'Água, tel. 289 543 674; www.quintadofreixo.org/quintadomel
- **Carpe Vita**, Rua Serra do Mosqueiro 36, Aljezur, tel. 963 256 581; www.carpe-vita.com; mid-July–mid-Sept (only rented by the week, Sat–Sat)
- **Monta da Vilarinha**, Vilarinha Bordeira, tel. 282 973 218 & 916 192 119; www.montedavilarinha.com; turn-off on the country highway from Vila do Bispo to Carrapateira
- **Aldeia da Pedralva**, Rua de Baixo, Casa da Pedralva, Vila do Bispo, tel. 282 639 342; www.aldeiadapedralva.com; turn-off on the country high-way from Vila do Bispo to Carrapateira

Tavira (➤ 66). Livestock farming and agriculture flourished here until the 1970s. They used to grow such crops as wheat and barley, and made a living from their stocks of fig, carob, olive and almond trees. Today, it's a flourishing hub of high-quality eco-tourism. The guest rooms and suites are decorated in a rustic style, the property is surrounded by a hilly, green, leafy landscape, and you can take a dip in the pool if you want to cool off. The grounds cover 120ha (96ac) and are ideal for bird-watching and short walks. There's a bar and a large veranda in the main house, and they'll serve you dinner if you book ahead. Somewhat closer to the sea – not far from the Praia da Falésia (➤ 92) and Vilamoura marina (➤ 103) – is the **Quinta do Mel**, a property in the central Algarve that deserves every one of its four stars. There's a pool at your disposal and they serve good meals.

Inland Accommodation

You'll also find beautiful lodgings if you head inland from the Costa Vicentina (➤ 153). Check out Aljezur, for example, where Luísa and Nuno Guimarães have set up **Carpe Vita** and renovated some traditional little cottages for self-caterers. They come with a small kitchen and have space for two to four people. You'll also have a pleasant stay in Casa Forno, Casa da Ribeira and Casas de Cima – the cottages at **Monte da Vilarinha** near Carrapateira. If you fancy something extraordinary, check out **Aldeia da Pedralva** in the municipality of Vila do Bispo (➤ 173), where some of the once-dilapidated houses have been transformed into tourist accommodation at great expense by António Ferreira and his wife Filipa. You can also eat in the partly over-hauled village that's criss-crossed with narrow, cobbled streets. The number of "locals" still living here is in single digits. It attracts a diverse group of guests, including couples of all ages, seniors and 👪 families with kids.

Turismo Rural is a great way to experience the Algarve's more rural side

HIKING on the
ROTA VICENTINA

If you love raw, wild, romantic scenery with spectacular views over the cliffs and want to get to know a piece of the inland Algarve, take a walk along a stretch of the Rota Vicentina, a long-distance hiking route in the west of the region. You'll have to be in pretty good shape – it's by no means an easy stroll!

The wind whips your face and the Atlantic crashes against the cliffs below. The landscape is filled with scrub, and the plants all around you have been buckled to the earth by storms. Taste the air – the scent of rockrose mingled with the tang of sea salt reaches your nose. These are the sights and smells you can look forward to on the Rota Vicentina as it runs in stages from the interior by Santiago do Cacém in the north, passes Odeceixe and heads on to the fabled Cabo de São Vicente (➤ 127) in the south. The Rota Vicentina is made up of two routes, the **Caminho Histórico** (Historical Way) and the **Trilho dos Pescadores** (Fishermen's Trail). The two variants complement each other and bring the trail's total length to a sizeable 350km (217mi).

If you choose your route carefully, you'll get to enjoy breath-taking views from such vantage points as the Torre de Aspa as you walk

HOMEPAGE, ACCOMMODATION, WALKING GUIDES

■ You'll find detailed descriptions of the route's various stages and other useful information on altitude gains, degrees of difficulty and estimated hiking times in English on the official Rota Vicentina homepage (visit www.rotavicentina.com). The maps on the website are interactive and the stage descriptions can be downloaded free of charge – they couldn't be more helpful if they tried!

Insider Tip

■ If you're confident of reaching your destinations on time each day, book your accommodation in advance. The Pensão das Dunas (Rua da Padaria 9, tel. 282 973 118 and 925 593 955; www.pensao-das-dunas.pt) and the Casa Fajara (CX 121P Vale de Carrapateira, Bordeira, tel. 282 973 134; www.casafajara.com) are good options in Carrapateira. For Vila do Bispo, check out the Hotel Mira Sagres (Rua 1° de Maio 3, tel. 282 639 160 and 925 408 080; www.hotelmirasagres.com).

■ Although it's quite possible to walk the Rota Vicentina on your own, you can also hire a local guide. (You might also want to limit yourself to a day-long hiking trip.) The best tour guide for miles around is Nicolau da Costa (Atalaia Walking, tel. 967 932 206; www.atalaia-walking.com). He speaks good English and knows this part of the Rota Vicentina better than almost anyone else.

Insider Tip

The Route to the Cape

Few people have time to walk the Rota Vicentina in its entirety. In any case, large sections of the trail extend out through the Alentejo region and beyond, far overstepping the geographic limits of this book. If you're in good shape, it's worth taking a multi-day hike through the Costa Vicentina

The Magazine

region and the Parque Natural do Sudoeste Alentejano e da Costa
Vicentina. Allow four days for the route. The starting point is the small
town of Aljezur (➤ 160). From there, head inland along the Historical Way
until you reach Arrifana by the coast (12km/7.5mi). From Arrifana, walk
on to Carrapateira (24km/15mi), where you'll find some accommodation
for the night. You'll want to take things a little easier after such a gruelling
walk, so stay in Carrapateira (➤ 163) and limit yourself to a 10km (6mi)
round-trip to see the cliffs and beaches along the Circuito Pontal de
Carrapateira, a loop of the Fishermen's Trail, the following day. You only
need to take a smaller backpack with you. Next morning, continue your
hike along the Historical Way from Carrapateira to Vila do Bispo (22km/
13.5mi), where you'll spend another two nights. From Vila do Bispo
(➤ 173), walk another 13km (8mi) along a combination of the Historical
Way and the Fishermen's Trail to the Cabo de São Vicente (➤ 127).
There's nowhere to stay at the Cape of St. Vincent itself, so head back
along the same 13km (8km) route to Vila do Bispo – this day-long round
trip only requires a small backpack. You'll be rewarded en route with
unforgettable views of one of the roughest and most beautiful cliff landscapes in southwestern Europe.

Tips for Hiking this Isolated Route

The Rota Vicentina is marked out with light blue/green trail markers.
Descriptions and signposts help you stick to the right path as you head
along the different stages of the route. Make sure your walking boots are
well broken in and have ankle support. Your backpack should be as light
as possible – under no circumstance should it weigh more than ten per
cent of your bodyweight. Take a tiny first aid kit with some blister plasters.
You'll also need to carry sun protection and a light rain cape with you.
Walking/telescopic poles can be helpful on the more difficult sections.
Make sure to take plenty of food and water, as the paths lead through
lonely terrain between settlements. It's absolutely beautiful, but there's
nothing to buy along the way.

**If you're hiking down an inland stretch of the Rota Vicentina, visit or stay overnight at
one of the wineries you come across (like this one near Aljezur)**

Golf Galore

The Algarve is a dream come true for golf fans. The region boasts a selection of more than three dozen courses that are open year round thanks to the favourable climate. The surrounding landscape ranges from seaside scenes to orange groves and adds an extra little kick to your game.

The strange, elongated pieces of luggage you'll spot shuffling along the carousels in Faro airport will give you an early inkling of the kind of place you've just flown to – this part of the Atlantic coast is a golfer's paradise! Experts praise the Algarve as one of the best golfing destinations in the world. It's already received awards and reached the top spot in various rankings, including those voted on by readers of "Today's Golfer", a British golfing magazine.

Tournaments and Championship Courses

Major tournaments featuring the stars of the international golfing scene are frequently played in the deep south of Portugal. The region boasts several championship courses as a result. Take the **Oceânico Victoria**, for example, a course set up by Arnold Palmer that has already played host to the Portugal Masters on several occasions. Or check out the **Oceânico Faldo Course** in Amendoeira, a links designed by British superstar Nick Faldo, three-time winner of the US Masters and one of the best European golfers of all time.

TOP SPOTS FOR GOLFERS

- **Penina Hotel & Golf Resort**, Penina, Portimão, tel. 282 420 200; www.penina.com
- **Alto Golf**, Quinta Alto do Vale, Quatro Estradas, Alvor, tel. 282 460 870; www.pestanagolf.com
- **Oceânico Victoria**, Vilamoura, tel. 289 310 333; www.oceanicogolf.com
- **Oceânico Faldo Course**, Amendoeira, tel. 289 310 333; www.oceanico golf.com
- **Silves Golf**, Vila Fria, Silves, tel. 282 440 130; www.pestanagolf.com
- **Oceânico Millennium**, Vilamoura, tel. 289 310 333; www.oceanicogolf.com
- **Quinta do Lago Golf**, Quinta do Lago, tel. 289 390 700; www.quintado lago.com

The Algarve's coastal cliffs provide great vantage points for golfers

Finessed and Multifaceted

The courses' difficulty levels, challenges and structural intricacies are as varied as the locations themselves, which range from spots on the coast to places further inland. Depending on the setup, they might boast water hazards, integrated wetlands and a varied plant life that includes umbrella pines and palm, orange, olive and carob trees. The natural silence is only broken by the occasional swish of a club.

The **Penina Championship Course** – designed by Sir Henry Cotton and dating back to the mid-1960s when Portugal was still under a dictatorship – is a legendary and unwaveringly popular links in the western Algarve. Although the Penina was the birthplace of golf in the region, the likes of the Oceânico and Pestana hotel groups have long provided some stiff competition. Despite their renown, not everyone is a fan of the region's courses, however: many are critical of their water consumption.

Attractive and Exclusive

Golf is a lucrative business and is sometimes associated with stays in top hotels. But playing here isn't as expensive as you might think – the green fees are excellent value considering what you get for your money. Many places offer golfing package holidays that include accommodation, green fees and meals. Golf schools are also available and the region's driving ranges and putting greens are of the highest standard. What's more, the Algarve is a great golfing destination in winter – in fact, the height of summer is its low season! And when you've finished playing, the club house terraces are an inviting place for a drink.

Finding Your Feet

First Two Hours

By Air

Many people travel to the Algarve via Faro airport. You can fly there from various destinations in the UK (carriers include easyJet, Ryanair and British Airways) and a number of European cities. A flight from London takes around 2.5 hours. There are far fewer connections in winter.

At Faro Airport

- **Faro Airport** *(Aeroporto de Faro)* lies around 6km (4mi) west of the city (tel. 289 800 800; www.ana.pt, e-mail: faro.airport@ana.pt).
- **City Bus Lines** 14 and 16 run between Faro and the airport (daily, 5am–11pm, tel. 289 899 760; www.proximo.pt, proximo@proximo.pt). A one-way bus journey costs €2.22 and it's €5.29 for a day ticket.
- The officially registered local **taxi companies** include Auto Faro (tel. 911 910 808 and 707 227 227; www.auto-faro.com) and Taxi Transfers Pinheiro (tel. 915 559 293; www.taxipinheiro.com). Both of these companies give you the option of booking a trip to your desired destination in advance via their websites. Bear in mind that they will charge a supplement for oversized luggage.

Rental Cars

- A number of **car rental companies** have branches at Faro Airport. It's well worth thinking about booking a car in advance – the prices are relatively high if you rent on arrival. What's more, pre-booking saves you time and makes sure you get the class of vehicle you want.
- Comparison sites like holidayautos.co.uk, easycar.com and travelsupermarket.com may help you find the best possible deals on a rental car. It can also sometimes be worth ringing up the major rental companies direct to see what sort of prices they have to offer.
- If you're looking to rent a car, make sure you're the **minimum required age**. You usually have to be 21 (and even 25 with some companies), and you must have been in possession of your driving licence for at least a year (your national driving licence is sufficient).
- It's vital to have a **credit card** when picking up a rental car.
- If you book far enough in advance in the low season, you can secure yourself a rental car from just €85–€90 **per week** including basic insurance coverage and unlimited mileage.
- Make absolutely sure that your rental car is equipped with a small **toll device**. This little box, which costs an extra €1.50–€2 per day to rent, electronically records all the fees you incur on the Algarve's major highway, the A22 (and on other motorways in Portugal). The A22 doesn't have any toll booths or other spots where you can pay by cash. Don't make the mistake of trying to save money by not renting a toll box – it's a false economy. The Algarve's national and country highways are completely unsuitable as alternatives to the main motorway when you need to get around more quickly (when rushing to catch your flight, for instance). The traffic on them is too tightly packed, especially during the high season, and you'll come up against speed restrictions and a great deal of traffic lights when you head through towns, etc.
- You'll find more **info about the toll** at www.visitportugal.com (hover over "All About Portugal" and click "Useful Information", then click "Read More" under "Electronic tolls" on the next page).

Getting Here over Land

- Taking a train or bus to the Algarve from other parts of Europe isn't a great alternative to flying – the journey times are staggering. Nevertheless, some people like to drive to the region via Spain in their own **car, motorbike or mobile home**. There are some fantastic places to stop off along the route – check out Barcelona and Madrid, the Atlantic coastal region and the province of Extremadura, for example. It's also possible to combine your trip to the Algarve with holidays in parts of Andalusia (e.g. Granada and Seville).

- Free **route planners** (e.g. www.viamichelin.co.uk) will help you calculate driving times and costs for fuel and toll roads. If you're dead set on this option, plan several days for your trip – it's around 2,500 kilometres (1,500 miles) from London to Faro, for example.

- Something to bear in mind if you're planning to drive from **Andalusia** via Ayamonte and over the Rio Guadiana border river on the motorway (the A49 in Spain that crosses over to the A22 in Portugal) – journeying on the **A22** incurs a **toll**. Unfortunately, you can only pay via **electronic sensor**, which is even more problematic if you have a foreign licence plate. As soon as you reach the A22, head over to the **electronic control point** on the right-hand side to register your license plate and your credit card info. Your card will then be charged according to the checkpoints and other toll stations you drive through.

- To spare your holiday budget, make sure to **fill your car up** with fuel before heading over the border from Spain into Portugal – it's significantly cheaper there!

Security

- The Algarve is basically a safe place to travel.

- If you're leaving any belongings in your car, lock them all up in the boot/trunk – never leave them lying inside the car itself. Even if your things have no value, the sight of them sitting there in full view can be tempting to would-be thieves.

- For security's sake, never leave your luggage unattended if you're queuing at a car rental counter or waiting for a bus.

- Pickpockets are uncommon, but can't be totally ruled out. Make life as difficult as possible for light fingered thieves: don't put your wallet in your back pocket or carry your rucksack on your back in crowds.

- Keep as little cash on you as possible – larger sums and important documents should be held in your hotel safe.

Tourist Information

- The first tourist information stand you'll come across is in Faro Airport (tel. 289 818 582). Faro's main office is found on the edge of the Old Town (Rua da Misericórdia 8–11, tel. 289 803 604; www.cm-faro.pt). The information you'll get at these offices is usually pretty basic. It's often limited to a large city map and a few brochures.

A NOTE ABOUT OPENING HOURS

The **opening hours** of tourist information offices, museums and attractions can change depending on the season (and sometimes at random!) Tourist information offices are often closed at weekends, regardless of what you might be told elsewhere. The times in this book should only be used as estimates.

Finding Your Feet

- **You'll find further tourist information offices** all over the Algarve, including in Albufeira, Alcoutim, Aljezur, Alvor, Armação de Pêra, Carvoeiro, Castro Marim, Lagos, Loulé, Monchique, Monte Gordo, Olhão, Portimão, Praia da Rocha, Quarteira, Sagres, São Brás de Alportel, Silves and Tavira.
- Tourist offices often carry the **"Algarve Guia/Guide"**, free monthly brochure that's printed in English and Portuguese. It gives visitors a good overview of the concerts, events, exhibitions, festivals, sports fixtures and markets taking place in the region. It's also posted online on the Algarve tourist board's official website (www..visitalgarve.pt).

Getting Around

With an area of around 5,000km² (3,100mi²), the Algarve might seem manageably sized at first glance, but don't assume you can drive from east to west in a hurry – it can be as far as 200km (125mi) from end to end. What's more, there isn't a continuous route along the coast – you can sometimes only get to beaches by taking long detours inland. The bus network is good, however, and there are regular trains.

By Car

- If you're in your **own car**, you'll need your driving licence, vehicle documents, proof of insurance and a nationality badge/sticker.
- **You have to any pay fines you incur on the spot**, otherwise your car may be confiscated by the police.
- Quite a lot has improved since the days when the Portuguese seemed to drive by feel. But don't get complacent: the locals' **driving style** can sometimes be very aggressive, particularly when they're overtaking. You won't be the first to notice that this doesn't quite fit in with their usual, rather laid-back mentality. If in doubt, drive defensively!

Traffic Rules

- The **speed limits** are 50km/h (30mph) in built-up areas, 90km/h (55mph) on country highways and 120km/h (74mph) on motorways.
- All drivers and passengers must **wear a seatbelt**.
- The **alcohol limit** for drivers is 0.05% blood alcohol content. The penalties for exceeding this limit are immense. If you have less than 3 years' driving experience, the limit is reduced to 0.02%.
- Unless otherwise stated, **give priority to traffic coming from the right.**
- Making **phone calls while you drive** is forbidden and is punishable with some pretty hefty fines. You are allowed to make calls on loudspeaker or using a handsfree kit, however.

Precautions for Motorists

- The Portuguese **double-laned roundabout** is a common source of **accidents**. Take particular care on them as some drivers like to veer off from the inside track (the fast lane) straight to the nearest exit without warning. A tip to prevent accidents: put your left indicator on continuously while on the roundabout until you want to exit from the outer lane.
- Signs marking **sections of road monitored by speed cameras** (velocidade controlada) should be taken very seriously. They might be a bluff, of course - but that's certainly not always the case! If you drive too quickly,

you'll sometimes find that the next set of traffic lights will turn red automatically to slow you down.

- Don't just drive straight into **villages with winding roads**. Instead, leave your car parked on the outskirts. Trying to drive through the streets in some villages – which can be narrow, steep and curving – isn't always good for your blood pressure!
- Never park too close to **coastal cliffs** - they're sometimes weakened by erosion. Some spots have warning signs..
- Always be on your guard in rural areas: **livestock** (cattle, sheep) and even **horses and carts** can suddenly appear in front of you.
- Don't underestimate dusty, stony tracks that head down to country houses and run through nature reserves. If it starts to rain (something that fortunately doesn't happen too often in the Algarve), these **tracks** can quickly turn into a mud bath.
- Some **roads in the interior** don't have a central reservation or crash barriers, so take great care when facing oncoming traffic. Side roads are sometimes also in poor condition (e.g. filled with potholes, etc.). The public funds needed to repair them are often lacking.
- Keep your eyes peeled for bark and branches lying in the road when driving through **wooded areas** (particularly under eucalyptus trees).
- Watch out for **cyclists on racing bikes**, especially at the weekend – some uncompromising people like to ride side-by-side in groups of two or three, creating danger for everyone involved. The roads in the Serra de Monchique leading up to Fóia are particularly popular with cyclists.

Further Hints and Tips for Drivers

- **Brown road signs** point to attractions, beaches and tourist sites. The drive there will usually be worth your while.
- Watch out for signs pointing to **paid parking zones** (zona pago, pay at ticket machines) in built-up areas. Other signs designate **residents' parking zones** (zona residentes).
- In towns like Faro, some poorer people work as self-appointed **parking attendants**. It's up to you if you want to give them some money or not.
- There's limited **parking space** near beaches and in smaller holiday resorts. U-turns and other manoeuvres can be difficult. It's better to park slightly further away.
- The **routes out of towns and cities** are sometimes only signposted with a single word: saída.
- **Passing places/lay-bys** are provided on some difficult roads.
- **The cheapest places to fill up on fuel** are supermarket petrol/gas stations (at Intermarché and Pingo Doce, for example).
- It can be worth driving to Spain to get fuel when you're in the eastern Algarve. You can fill up much more cheaply there.
- There are some petrol/gas stations that require **payment in advance** (pré-pagamento).

Buses & Trains

You can get to a selection of destinations very easily by bus or train. Having a (rental) car is your only option if you want to visit some more remote villages and beaches, however. Public transport is cheaper here than in many other parts of Europe.

- **Eva Transportes** is a major bus company in the Algarve. Tel. 289 589 055 and 289 513 616; www.eva-bus.com. (Visit their website for an easy way to search for bus connections.)

Finding Your Feet

- Eva Transportes offer a **tourist pass** *(passe turístico)* that gives visitors unlimited travel in the Algarve for one fixed price. You can get your hands on a tourist pass for three days (€29.10) or an entire week (€36.25).
- **Frota Azul** is another of the Algarve's bus companies (tel. 282 400 610 and 282 418 120; www.frotazul-algarve.pt). It provides services along such routes as Portimão–Monchique and Portimão–Lagos.
- You'll find a central **bus station** *(terminal rodoviário)* in such larger towns as Albufeira, Tavira and Olhão.
- The regional **train network** runs from Vila Real de Santo António in the east to Lagos in the west. Visit www.cp.pt for routes and prices.
- Some of the trains look a little old-fashioned, and some stations no longer have ticket counters or information desks. If that's the case, you can buy **tickets** from the conductor on the train at no extra cost.
- You're usually allowed to **transport bikes** in the luggage cars of trains. You don't have to pay any extra to take them with you.

Taxis

- Taxis are beige or black/green and have a **sign** that says "Taxi" in full view up on the roof.
- You'll find **taxi ranks** in many places. You'll sometimes have to pay extra if you want to order a taxi by phone.
- Make sure that the **taximeter** is turned on.
- **You'll usually pay extra** for journeys taken between 9pm and 6am and on weekends.
- Boat shuttles take people to the island beaches in the Ria da Formosa nature reserve – they're known as **boat taxis** *(taxis maritimos)*.

Accommodation

There's a wide selection of accommodation available in the Algarve, ranging from hotels and apartments to B&Bs, country houses and campsites. Take your budget and the needs of your guests (e.g. their desired location and level of comfort) into consideration when making your choice.

Bookings

- You can try making **direct bookings** on the websites of the accommodation you're interested in. Whatever you do, make sure to compare the prices in advance! You'll sometimes get better rates from such **booking sites** as www.booking.com and www.hrs.com. If you're planning to stay in one place, a package holiday deal might be a better option.
- The **pricing structure** is often very broad and very flexible. Rates are prone to constant fluctuation, sometimes changing several times a week depending on supply and demand.
- **Online bookings** are almost always cheaper than booking at reception. Even if you've just arrived and want somewhere to stay that night, book online on your phone before walking into the hotel!
- Make sure to book well in advance if you're staying in the Algarve's **high season** (July and August). You should also book ahead for accommodation during school holidays and local festivals.
- You can book and take a good look at **holiday homes and apartments** on sites like www.atraveo.com.

General Tips

- **Breakfast** *(pequeno almoço)* is often – but not always – included in the price of your accommodation.
- The southern **tempo of life** means that the day starts a little later here: breakfast only kicks off at 8am in some places.
- **VAT (Value Added Tax)** should be included in all quoted room prices.
- You're often required to pay **extra** for indoor parking spots at hotels. Whether or not you'll also have to pay more for wireless Internet and sports and health facilities depends on the place.
- Travel outside the **high season** if you can – your accommodation might cost half or even a third of the normal price. A two-person apartment that's €130 in July/Aug can cost just €45 in Nov, Jan or Feb!
- Some accommodation offers wheelchair-accessible rooms.
- You can sometimes only **check in** from 4pm. You'll need to **check out** again by noon at the latest.

Hotels and B&Bs

- Hotels are ranked from one to five **stars** (depending on facilities).
- Due to rising guest expectations, some top-class places now offer a **fitness suite** and a **spa** with a sauna, indoor pool and steam room alongside the usual open-air swimming pool (**extra charges** may apply).
- **Vila Galé** (www.vilagale.com) is one of the best loved, highest-quality hotel chains in the upper price bracket. You'll find their hotels in and around Tavira, Vilamoura, Albufeira, Armação de Pêra and Lagos.
- **Pousadas** (www.pousadas.pt) are hotels, many of which have been set up in historic buildings. Check out their places in Tavira (a former monastery) and Estoi (a former aristocratic palace) when you're in the Algarve. There's also a third Pousada in Sagres.
- Some hotel resorts come with **golf courses**.
- If you don't want to stay in a hotel, try the simpler accommodation at **guest houses** *(estalagem, hospedaria)* and **inns** *(residencial, pensião)* for size. They don't usually serve any meals beyond breakfast.

Apartments

- Apartments and houses for **self-caterers** are widespread. They're usually well equipped and suitable for ██ families with kids. Fridges and simple hot plates (sometimes run on bottles of butane gas) come as standard. Depending on the place you choose, you might also get a microwave, a kettle/coffee machine, a washing machine and/or a dryer.
- **Communal facilities** often include a swimming pool, a kids' pool and some open green spaces.
- Check to see whether or not your accommodation comes with **air conditioning** (or heating in winter!) and a balcony or terrace.
- Some **campsites** also rent out apartments.

Tourism in the Countryside

- If you fancy escaping the hustle and bustle of the coast and want to get closer to nature, rent a room in a **rural guesthouse**. Some of them are found on farms and estates.
- Country lodgings are usually **family-run**. You'll have lots of contact with your hosts, who can often give you tips for your stay.
- **Directions** for getting to rural accommodation are often complicated if you're not familiar with the area. Make sure to download/print out a route description and/or a map from their websites before you arrive.

Finding Your Feet

Accommodation Prices
for a double room per night in the high season
€ under €90   €€ €90–€150   €€€ over €150

- A few key words in Portuguese can be of great help when you're **googling** information about country tourism. Try *Agroturismo, Turismo Rural, Turismo de Habitação, Casas de Campo*.
- If you're looking for **rural accommodation** (➤ 40) on the **Costa Vicentina** (around Aljezur and Carrapateira, for example), you'll find numerous options on the website of the **Casas Brancas** rental association (www.casasbrancas.pt/en).

Youth Hostels

- Travellers on a budget might like to make use of **youth hostels** *(pousadas de juventude)*. The price for a bed in a shared dorm will cost around €10–€17, depending on the season. A double room with a bathroom will cost around €28–€45.
- You'll only find youth hostels in a few parts of the Algarve, including Lagos, Faro, Tavira and Portimão.
- You can get more information and make bookings on the homepage of the **Portuguese Youth Hostel Association** (https://juventude.gov.pt/) or via **Hostelling International** (www.hihostels.com).

Camping

- **Campsites** *(parques de campismo)* provide pitches for tents, caravans and motorhomes. They also frequently offer small cottages, apartments or static caravans to rent.
- Various **websites** can help you search for campsites. Check out www.camping.info and www.eurocampings.co.uk, for example. There's also www.roteiro-campista.pt if you don't mind tackling some Portuguese.

Food and Drink

When it comes to dining, they do things differently in the Algarve. As well as some unique culinary specialities (➤ 34), their restaurants have unfamiliar mealtimes, put appetisers on the table as you arrive, serve lots of two-person dishes, and often provide slower service than at home...

Mealtimes

- **Breakfast** *(pequeno almoço)* – a meal the locals don't really make a song and dance about – is usually served from 7:30am, although some places only provide breakfast from 8am, and a few country houses don't get started until 8:30/9:00am. Despite the locals' apathy, hotels often have extensive breakfast buffets for their foreign clientele.
- **Lunch** *(almoço)* is served from around noon/12:30 to 2/2:30pm.
- **Dinner** *(jantar)* is served from around 7/7:30pm–8pm in some places. It usually lasts until around 10/10:30pm.
- Many restaurants have **non-stop service** and continuous opening hours, particularly during the summer season.

Restaurants

■ There isn't usually any strict sense of etiquette in restaurants – just don't turn up barefoot, in your swimming costume or looking completely dishevelled. You can get away with more casual clothing in informal beach restaurants, however.

■ The best restaurants – the places where locals flock to eat **good food at low prices** – often don't look very inviting or anything like the kind of standard you might be used to at home. Don't be too picky, however – if it's full of locals, you've come to the right spot! There sometimes won't even be a menu with a list of prices. The Portuguese tend to be honest, however, so you can (almost!) always safely assume you'll pay the right price at the end of your meal.

■ It's polite to let the waiting staff **show you to your table** instead of taking the initiative and finding one yourself.

■ Restaurant owners in the Algarve know that they won't just be serving Portuguese guests. For that reason, most have **menus in English** (just don't expect tip-top spelling or grammatical perfection!)

■ *Marisqueiras* are what the locals call restaurants specialising in **fish and seafood**. It's absolutely fine to use your hands when you're eating cockles or other shellfish.

■ It's advisable to **book a table in advance** in the high season. This isn't always possible at some simple restaurants, however. If that's the case, you'll just have to wait in line or at the bar for a seat.

■ If you want to pay by **credit card** *(cartão de crédito)*, find out if it's accepted before you eat. You might have difficulties paying with plastic in some of the region's more basic eateries.

■ Restaurants generally have a **day off** (and sometimes also an evening off) every week, although many people work every single day during the summer season. You'll also find that some restaurants close their doors completely during the winter months.

■ Whether a **set menu** includes drinks or not will depend on the restaurant. If in doubt, ask before you order.

■ It's not unheard of for the **service** in restaurants to be a lot slower than you might be used to at home. It's probably just because the kitchen and the staff are temporarily overwhelmed. If this is the case, getting heated or complaining won't help matters at all. Try relaxing into the Portuguese swing of things: practise a little patience and enjoy another glass of something tasty while you wait!

■ You should **tip** around 5–10 per cent, depending on how happy you were with your experience.

Specialities

■ Like all southerners, the local *Algarvios* take a very long time over their main meals. Meals aren't just a time to eat, after all – they're a chance for everyone to get together and socialise.

■ Garlic, olive oil and coriander are common components of southern Portuguese cuisine.

■ **Butter** comes either salted *(manteiga com sal)* or unsalted *(manteiga sem sal)*.

■ The *Algarvios* like to eat **soup** first, e.g. fish soup *(sopa de peixe)*, vegetable soup *(sopa de legumes)*, cream of tomato soup *(creme de tomate)* or *caldo verde*, a soup from the north of Portugal that's made with cabbage, potatoes and a little pork sausage *(chouriço)*. The soup of the day *(sopa do dia)* is always good value.

Finding Your Feet

- The light bites that are known as *tapas* in neighbouring Spain are called **petiscos** in Portugal.
- Common **snacks** include toasties *(tostadas)* and sandwiches *(sandes)* – a pork sandwich *(bifana)* is a popular choice.
- If you order a set menu, you'll sometimes find that the sides accompanying your main course seem a little meagre compared to your starter.
- When it comes to **desserts** *(sobremesas)* and patisserie, people in the Algarve (and all over Portugal) have a very sweet tooth. Popular choices include a piece of chocolate cake *(bolo de chocolate)*, a slice of apple tart *(tarte de maça)*, a portion of almond cake *(tarte de amêndoa)* or some rice pudding *(arroz doce)*. For a healthier option, opt for a fruit salad *(salada de frutas)*.

Eating in Restaurants

- Perhaps the most distinctive feature of the region's restaurants is the **table setting**. This often includes an array of invitingly presented appetisers: as well as bread *(pão)* and butter *(manteiga)*, you'll frequently see pickled olives *(azeitonas)*, sardine paste *(pasta de sardinha)*, tuna paste *(pasta de atum)* and/or a piece of cheese *(queijo)*. Anything you eat or try will have to be paid for at the end of your meal. If you don't touch something you haven't ordered, you won't be charged for it when it's time to settle up.
- Restaurants usually offer a simple, reasonably priced set lunch menu or **dish of the day** *(prato do dia)* around noon. The set menu might consist of two to three courses and cost just €8–€10.
- They'll sometimes also provide a **kids' menu** *(menu de criança)*.
- When it comes to fish, the chalk boards and menus in restaurants will often only tell you they're serving the **fresh fish of the day** *(peixe fresco do dia)*. Just ask if you want to know exactly what they have in stock.
- You'll often find that the more elaborate dishes served in the Algarve's restaurants can only be ordered for **two people** – e.g. monkfish rice *(arroz de tamboril)*, octopus rice *(arroz de polvo)* and seafood rice *(arroz de marisco)*. Most dishes cooked in a typical copper pot *(cataplana)* – e.g. a cataplana fish stew with cockles and shrimps *(cataplana de peixe com amêijoas e camarão)* – are also only served to dining duos. You'll have to fork out around €28–€45 for a two-person dish in a low to mid-priced restaurant.
- Restaurants of all shapes and sizes will sometimes sell fish and other foods (e.g. high quality shrimp and even veal cutlets) **by the kilo**. Be careful – the price can soon mount up!
- Unless you've fallen into a bit of a tourist trap, the portions you'll be given in the Algarve's restaurants will be very generous indeed. À la carte main dishes are sometimes served in **whole portions** *(dose)* and **half portions** *(meia dose)*. The half portions cost around two thirds of the whole price and will often be enough to fill you up.
- If you can't decide what to have, just ask for a **recommendation from the chef** *(sugestão do chefe)*!
- If you can't choose which **fish dish** you'd like, it's always a good idea to try the fish stew *(caldeirada de peixe)* or a mixed seafood platter.
- **Dried salt-cod** *(bacalhau)* is served everywhere and prepared in hundreds of different ways. You'll find it all over Portugal, however, so it's not particularly typical of the Algarve. Although you'll often spot it on the menu, **salmon** *(salmão)* is usually imported from countries in much more northerly climes.

> **Restaurant Prices**
> for a three-course set menu without drinks or service:
> € under €20   €€ €20–€35   €€€ over €35

- A **mixed salad** *(ensalada mista)* is often a very reasonably priced option.
- More and more restaurants **now serve vegetarian meals** *(pratos vege-tarianos)*. If they don't, however, the veggies among you might find yourselves stuck with a choice between an omelette *(omelete)* and an empty stomach.

Drinks

- **Mineral water** is the most common drink in the Algarve. It comes in still *(agua sem gás)* and bubbly *(agua com gás)* varieties. You'll also usually be asked whether you'd like to have it served chilled *(fresca)* or at room temperature *(natural)*. "Pedras Salgadas" is regarded as the best brand of fizzy water on the market.
- No main meal would be complete without a drop or two of good wine. Even the locals enjoy drinking the **house wine** *(vinho da casa)* in restau-rants – you'll often find it comes straight from the Algarve itself. If you'd prefer a tipple from another part of the country, try a red *(vinho tinto)* from the Alentejo or the Douro Valley or a white *(vinho branco)* from Beiras or Trás-os-Montes. "Green wine" *(vinho verde),* a young wine from the Minho valley, is a fruity, slightly fizzy alternative.
- All **good quality wine** has a protected designation of origin *(denominação de origem)* displayed on the label. **Port** from the north of Portugal is available all over the Algarve, and can be enjoyed as an aperitif or with dessert. For a particularly classy drink, try *tawny* port.
- **Beer** *(cerveja)* is also popular – try a "Sagres", for example.
- Portuguese people will happily drink an **espresso** *(café*; also called *bica,* the term from Lisbon and the surrounding area) at any time of day, and not just to round off their meal. They're very cheap (around €0.60). A **latte** *(galão)* costs more, and is always served in a glass.
- Fancy one for the road? Try a typical **strawberry tree brandy** *(aguardente de medronho* or *medronho* for short). It's quite expensive and hits home hard. **Sour cherry liqueur** *(ginjinha)* is very sweet and fruity.

Shopping

Forget the identical mass-produced goods you'll see for sale at many of the shops in Albufeira and Carvoeiro – there's still some very beautiful pottery made by hand in the Algarve if you want a proper memento. Products made from cork and cork leather are also extremely attractive. And don't forget to stock up on culinary souvenirs!

Opening Times

- **Shops** generally open Mon–Sat, 9/10am–1pm and 3–7pm. Some close on Saturday afternoons. There are many exceptions to this rule, how-ever – it would be disastrous to close early and let sales slip away during

Finding Your Feet

the summer season. Some shops in tourist hotspots don't shut for lunch in the warmer months, and others have late opening hours and stay open on Sundays.

- **Supermarkets** are open from 9am–8/9pm every day. Modern **shopping centres** (with boutiques, shoe shops, etc.) open even longer thanks to the restaurants and cinemas you'll also find there.
- As well as the local supermarkets, you'll spot some international names you might recognise (e.g. Intermarché, Aldi, Iceland and Spar).

Crafts

It's not always easy to distinguish between junk and quality goods, but you'll get an eye for it with a bit of practice.

- **Ceramics** are still produced in places like Loulé, where they make plates, bowls, cups and even the odd ornamental fish for your wall. A decorated tile *(azulejo)* can be bought for as little as €5.
- **Cork** is used for coasters and photo frames, for example.
- Designers also avail themselves of **cork leather** (➤ 34) to create some chic accessories, purses and bags, etc.

Markets

- *Algarvios* love their traditional markets, whether they're held indoors or out. Self-caterers can also use them as a reliable place to stock up on the best quality goods. The prices are very low if you buy according to the season, what's being harvested, and the current fishing cycles. The largest and most beautiful **market halls** are in Olhão and Loulé. You'll also find **flea and junk markets** *(feiras de velharias)* all over the Algarve. They often run on fixed dates once or twice a month and are usually busiest during the morning – they frequently close around 1pm. Ask at a tourist office for the latest dates or have a search for them on the Internet.
- Flea and junk markets sell everything under the sun, ranging from kitsch to clothes. They're good places for finding ceramics, kitchenware, cork, wicker, wood and leather goods. Check to see you're **getting a good price for the quality you're buying** and don't let the holiday spirit carry you off into a spending frenzy.

Insider Tip
- Even if you don't want to buy anything, you shouldn't leave without experiencing the colourful hustle and bustle of the markets!

Culinary Souvenirs

- If you've travelled here in your own car or have space for a few bottles on the plane, think about buying an **Algarve wine** or a slightly pricey **strawberry tree brandy** *(medronho)*.
- Bottles of **olive oil** are also a good option. For the best quality, go for cold pressed olive oil *(azeite de oliva extravirgem)*.
- **Cheese** *(queijo;* sheep's milk cheese: *queijo de ovelha;* goat's cheese: *queijo de cabra)* and **hard-cured sausages** *(chouriços)* are easy to transport, but shouldn't be left in their packaging for too long!
- Markets are also good, cheap places to find jars of **honey** (try some rosemary or orange blossom honey, for example). Check to make sure the lid of the jar closes well before you transport it anywhere! Salted almonds, biscuits, baked goods, pickled olives, bottles of hot piri piri sauce, jams, chutneys, spices and little bags of herbs all make popular culinary souvenirs from the market.
- Holidaymakers like to buy the **salt** that's harvested in the Algarve by evaporating seawater in salt pans (e.g. near Castro Marim). As well as

table salt, you'll find packets of classy crystalline *flor de sal* ("flowers of salt") – it's much cheaper here than anywhere else.

More Shopping Tips

- **Leather shoes** are much cheaper in Portugal than elsewhere. Nevertheless, take the same amount of care you normally would when buying cheap or budget clothes: once you're back home, you won't have the chance to complain about faulty or poor quality goods!

- Consider buying one of the lidded, sealable **copper pans** *(cataplana)* that locals use to cook up some delicious dishes. They're typical of the Algarve, but difficult to transport.

- **Smaller, more lightweight souvenirs** include dishcloths, napkins, kitchen aprons and potholders emblazoned with a picture of the **Rooster of Barcelos**. This is a very typical Portuguese motif that harks back to the story of a pilgrim who, according to a traditional legend (▶ 85), arrived in the northern town of Barcelos and miraculously survived a very sticky situation thanks to a rooster's timely cry. You'll find a particularly large selection of these products in Vila Real de Santo António. Tablecloths, towels and clothes of all kinds are also sold there in the numerous shops downtown.

Entertainment

Although the nightlife isn't exactly buzzing in some places (which makes them absolutely perfect if you're looking for a bit of peace and quiet!), other towns offer plenty of choice if you want to party the night away.

Nightlife Hints and Tips

- Albufeira and Faro are **top spots for nightlife** in summer, followed by Praia da Rocha, Lagos and – to a lesser extent – Tavira.

- You'll see an international crowd painting the town red during the high season. They aren't afraid to prove their **drinking prowess**. This can make it easier to get to know new people or make them much more irritating, depending on your point of view.

- **Faro** is also a lively place to go out during the rest of the year thanks to its student population. Check out the **Rua do Crime**.

- Some of the Algarve's clubs and discos don't really get going until after 11pm or even **midnight** in summer.

- Bands play **live music** in some of the bars and clubs.

- The **marina** in **Vilamoura** is a nightlife hotspot.

- You'll sometimes also stumble across fado evenings and fado concerts. **Fado** is like the Portuguese version of the Blues. It comes from Lisbon but is known throughout the country. Its musical themes include love, longing and various kinds of heartache. A singer is usually accompanied by two guitarists. In some restaurants, fado is played while you eat your evening meal.

Sporting Pursuits

- The Algarve is a paradise for sports fans, and offers **golf courses, cycle routes, hiking trails, riding centres** and **water sports** galore; the latter include diving, standup paddleboarding, surfing, kite surfing and sea

Finding Your Feet

kayak tours that let you explore the rocky coasts from a new perspective. Some resorts also have tennis courts, volleyball, etc.

- The region's **long-distance hiking trails** include the 300km (185mi) **Via Algarviana** (www.via-algarviana.com), which stretches between Alcoutim and the Cabo de São Vicente, and the **Rota Vicentina** (▶ 42; www.rota vicentina.com), which measures in at around 350km (220mi) in length. Long-distance hiking trips require two things: a good level of fitness and careful planning. The first thing to think about is your backpack, which definitely shouldn't weigh more than 10kg (22lbs). An even better maximum to stick to is ten per cent of your bodyweight. If you want basic tips on what to pack, check out the Via Algarviana's website (www. via-algarviana.com).
- A **long-distance cycle route**, the 214km (133mi) **Ecovia** (a.k.a. Ecovia Litoral), runs from the Cabo de São Vicente in the west to Vila Real de Santo António (a town by the Rio Guadiana border river) in the east.
- **Surf camps** are held on the Costa Vicentina and elsewhere.
- **Diving** is possible on over 300 days a year. You'll find the **Ocean Revival** (www.oceanrevival.pt) underwater park to the east of Alvor. They've sunk some shipwrecks there especially for divers to explore.
- The **Algarve's International Autodrome** (Autódromo Internacional Algarve; www.autodromodoalgarve.com) lies inland from the coast near Portimão. It's deep in debt, but has managed to survive so far. The complex includes a go-kart facility and an off-road park.

Leisure Activities

- 🔢 **Dolphin Watching** (▶ 39) is a particularly popular activity for families with children in tow.
- If you're looking for **theatre and concerts** in Faro, check out the Teatro das Figuras (www.teatrodasfiguras.pt) and the Teatro Lethes (www. actateatro.org.pt/teatrolethes). The local **cultural centre** (Centro Cultural, Casa da Cultura) is also always a good place to start.
- The **Museu do Traje** (www.museu-sbras.com) in São Brás de Alportel occasionally holds such events as jazz concerts, fado performances and demonstrations of traditional dance (usually on Sundays).
- **Cinemas** are sometimes found at shopping complexes. Films are usually shown in their original language with Portuguese subtitles (one of the reasons why the Portuguese speak pretty good English!)
- In the warmer months of the year, the **Galeria Arte Algarve** (www.arte algarve.net) art gallery in Lagoa provides a stage for a large summer exhibition complete with a selection of accompanying events. A second branch of the Galeria Arte Algarve is found in Ferragudo – it's open until late at night in summer.

Festivals and Summer Events

- **Major events** include the Algarve Cup for women's football (some time in March) and the MED music festival held in Loulé in June.
- There are also **gastronomic festivals** like the Sardine Festival (Festival da Sardinha) in Portimão and the Seafood Festival (Festival do Marisco) in Olhão (both of which take place around mid-August).
- The 🔢 **International Sand Sculpture Festival** (Festival Internacional de Escultura em Areia; www.fiesa.org) is held in Pêra every year between late March and mid-October.
- Many towns and communities organise diverse **summer event programmes** in the high season with lots of fun activities.

Eastern Algarve

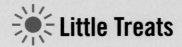 **Little Treats**

Lagoon Living
Head to the promenade in **Santa Luzia** (➤ 80) in the evening to soak up the the special atmosphere by the lagoon.

Singing the Blues
Fado, Portugal's Blues, can be heard at concerts held by the **Fado com História** (➤ 86) cultural association in **Tavira**.

Rest in Peace
This might be an unusual tourist tip, but it's worth visiting the typical Portuguese cemetery in **Cacela Velha** (➤ 79).

Getting Your Bearings

The eastern part of Portugal's sunny southern region is known as the *Sotavento algarvio* – the "leeward Algarve". It's famous for its impressive sandy beaches that run seamlessly into one another around Manta Rota and Monte Gordo. The region isn't completely unspoilt (you'll see some hulking concrete edifices behind the beaches, particularly in Monte Gordo), but there are still some isolated, unblemished spots to be found – check out the fragrant pine forests nearby and large swathes of the Ilha de Tavira, an island that's part of the Parque Natural da Ria Formosa (➤ 108).

Families with kids will have a great time going shell hunting on the 🔞 **Ilha de Tavira's long, sandy beach**. People usually reach the island from **Tavira**, the most attractive and diverse town in the region. Tavira's justified reputation is based on its selection of good eateries and special cultural sites, including the Igreja da Misericórdia, a church in the Old Town that's covered in azulejos. Right out east is the **Rio Guadiana**, a boundary river that marks the border with Spain and flows past the castle town of **Alcoutim**, the small **Reserva Natural do Sapal** nature reserve and **Vila Real de Santo António**, a lively city that's a good place to shop. The latter is the starting point for charming river trips along the Rio Guadiana. The region also boasts such gems as the village of **Cacela Velha** and the salt marshes around **Castro Marim** that are home to flamingos and other birds. One thing's for sure – you won't be bored in the eastern Algarve!

The lagoon by Cacela Velha

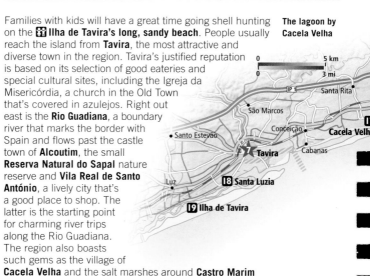

An architectural highlight: Tavira's Roman Bridge

Sardines from the grill are a tasty summer treat

Three Perfect Days

Although the eastern Algarve is largely known for its beaches, the region is also home to some interesting towns, villages and water parks. Our suggested itinerary will show you how to see the area's most important treasures in just three days. It assumes you have a (rental) car to get around. The best base to explore from is Tavira and the surrounding area.

Day One

Morning
Start your voyage of discovery in ⭐Tavira (➤ 66, image right), one of the most beautiful towns in the Algarve. Set aside enough time to take a stroll along the river, walk through the town's historic district, and visit all the most important sights (e.g. the Igreja da Misericórdia, the Camera Obscura and the small castle). Have lunch at one of Tavira's plentiful selection of restaurants.

Afternoon
Take a trip on the shuttle boat that ferries you from Tavira to the **19 Ilha de Tavira** (➤ 80). Spend a little while relaxing on the island in the afternoon sun before strolling along the beach. Afterwards, make your way back into Tavira itself.

Evening
When it's nearing dinner time, try driving southwest of Tavira to the nice, unspoilt village of **18 Santa Luzia** (➤ 80). It's a centre of octopus fishing that boasts a selection of good restaurants and an inviting harbour promenade. If you fancy a drink later at night, head back into Tavira – it's very atmospheric in the evening. The view of the bridge is enchanting after dark.

Day Two

Morning
Start the day by driving inland to **11 Alcoutim** (➤ 72), where you can visit the castle and look out over the Rio Guadiana into neighbouring Spain. Afterwards, head down south to Foz de Odeleite along the ⭐Rio Guadiana (➤ 70) river before driving all the way to **13 Vila Real de Santo António** (➤ 76). Take a lovely stroll through the bustling town centre to build up an appetite before settling down to enjoy a spot of lunch.

Afternoon
After your meal, walk a little way along the Rio Guadiana before driving to **12 Castro Marim** (➤ 74) that sits next to the salt marshes. Get yourself pumped up for battle and storm the castle (although non-violent visits are also encouraged!) before treating yourself to a rest by the cooling Atlantic – try the beach at **16 Manta Rota** (➤ 79).

Evening

The village of **17** **Cacela Velha** (➤ 79) is your destination for the evening. Stroll through the pretty streets and enjoy the view over parts of the **Parque Natural da Ria Formosa** (➤ 108). Stop somewhere for dinner.

Day Three

Morning/Afternoon

If you want to get to know the ★**8** **Rio Guadiana** (➤ 70) and the surrounding landscape a little better, book a day trip in **13** **Vila Real de Santo António** (➤ 76) from an operator like Riosultravel (www.riosultravel.com). The tour lasts from around 10am to 5pm. You'll drive part of the route overland and travel the rest aboard a river boat. Lunch is included in the price.

Evening

After heading back to Vila Real de Santo António, drive to **15** **Monte Gordo** (➤ 79) on the Atlantic coast. Ignore the concrete architectural monstrosities – the promenade and the beach are beautiful! Enjoying a bite to eat here is a great way to round off your day.

Alcoutim **11**

Rio Guadiana **8** ★

Reserva Natural do Sapal **14**

Castro Marim **12** Vila Real de Santo António **13**

Manta Rota **16** Monte Gordo **15**

Tavira ★ Cacela Velha **17**

18 Santa Luzia

19 Ilha de Tavira

Eastern Algarve

☆Tavira

Tavira is a city on the banks of the Rio Séqua/Rio Gilão that's home to 13,000 inhabitants. Its atmosphere and historical significance make it a true highlight of the eastern Algarve. It's a place of churches, river promenades, quiet old streets and lots of little treats that are just waiting to be discovered.

The **Praça da República** is a good place to start exploring the city. It's here you'll find a tourist information centre and can take a walk along the **Ponte Romano** ("Roman Bridge"). This impressive structure, the low arches of which span the Rio Gilão, is reserved for pedestrians. It's a good look-out point from which to admire the surrounding cityscape.

Insider Tip
On the other side of the bridge is a nice **nightlife and restaurant zone** around the Rua Dr. Antonio Cabreira, the Rua 5 de Outobro and the Praça Dr. Padinha. Take note of some of the eateries here – they're particularly inviting at night when the bridge's lanterns are illuminated. Slightly confusingly, the name of the river changes from **Rio Séqua** to **Rio Gilão** when it reaches the bridge.

Prosperous and Populous

The impressive houses along the river cast attractive reflections onto the water. These buildings from a bygone era hark back to a time when Tavira was a truly prosperous place. Although its castle and harbour had lent it a strategic significance under Islamic rule, it was not until the 16th century that Tavira became the Algarve's most populous city and really began to enhance its prestige.

Over time, the city's prosperity gave rise to the **richly decorated, sloping-roofed manor houses** and **numerous churches** that still dominate the cityscape today and make Tavira something of an open-air architectural museum. The facades covered in **azulejos** are a particularly eye-catching sight. Tavira's good fortune was not fated to last forever – an outbreak of the plague, the progressive silting up of the channel to the sea and the earthquake of 1755 all took their toll. Things started looking up again later on with the advent of tuna fishing, the fish canning industry and tourism, however. Although Tavira isn't by the sea, it's a good base for exploring the **Ilha de Tavira** (➤ 80) and its beautiful beaches thanks to the water-ways in the **Parque Natural da Ria Formosa** (➤ 108).

If you want to delve a little deeper into the history

Azulejos were used to create the expressive scenes that adorn Tavira's Igreja da Misericórdia

An atmospheric evening on the Praça da República by the steps of the Ponte Romana

of the centuries of Moorish rule in the region, visit the **Núcleo Museológico Islâmico**, the small Islamic Museum on the Praça da República. The exhibits housed in the collection's display cabinets include various jars and vessels with handles, fragments of painted ceramics and the *Vaso de Tavira*, a particularly elaborate medieval pot that was unearthed by archaeologists. The era of Islamic rule is also said to have rubbed off on the name of the city itself: *Tabara* – which gradually morphed into *Tabira* and then *Tavira* – meant something akin to "hidden".

Strolling through the Old Town

Take a short stroll away from the Praça da República and walk beside the river bank and some green open spaces to the former **Mercado da Ribeira**, a late-19th-century market hall. Take a rest stop on the benches under the palm trees and relax by the old bandstand. Then wend your way to the magnificent **Igreja da Misericórdia** (16th c.), one of Tavira's collection of over 20 churches.

Experts rightly regard this church as one finest Renaissance buildings to be found anywhere in the Algarve. The ornate facade is crowned by a figure of the Virgin Mary, *Nossa Senhora da Misericórdia*. The lower areas inside the church are decorated with azulejos – the scenes they show depict themes of Christian charity. The golden altarpiece – a typical example of the Portuguese *Talha dourada* gilded wood-carving technique – is equally eye-catching.

Historical Flair

If you walk a little further up through the historic district, you'll find yourself at the **Palácio da Galeria**, a Baroque palace that's been turned into a museum. Glass cases in

the entrance area show traces of the region's Phoenician past and the cult of the deity Baal. The ever-changing exhibition at the **Museu Municipal** (Municipal Museum) is somewhat less impressive.

Go further up the hill in the Old Town to find the **castelo**, a small, turreted medieval castle that boasts a well-kept, miniature botanic garden where you can admire some beautiful bougainvilleas, hibiscuses and other types of plant. It's worth visiting the castle (open every day and freely accessible) just to see this lovely garden alone. You can also enjoy some fantastic views over Tavira's tiled roofs and chimneys from the fortifications.

Another church worth seeing opposite the castle is the Gothic **Igreja de Santa Maria do Castelo**, which was probably built on the site of the former principal mosque. Once inside, your eyes will be drawn to the impressive white arches, azulejos, oil paintings and the high altar featuring a statue of the Virgin Mary wearing a crown. The church is the final resting place of Paio Peres Correia (1205–1275) – a Grand Master of the Order of Santiago – and the "Seven Knights" from the same Order who are said to have lost their lives in the fight against the Moors. The electric candles you can "light" look a little out of place. The tiny **Museu de Arte Sacra** (Museum of Sacred Art) adjoins the church itself.

INSIDER INFO

- You'll find the **camera obscura** in the former Torre de Tavira water tower up on the hill in Tavira's Old Town (Calçada da Galeria 12, Mon–Fri, 10am–4/5, Sat 10am–1pm; times vary slightly depending on the season; €4). Live images of Tavira are projected onto a screen in a dark room via a mirror and two lenses on the roof. These unusual views, which stretch all the way over to the salt marshes outside town, are also interesting for 👪 families with kids.

- 8km (5mi) east of Tavira lies the village of **Cabanas de Tavira**, which you can reach by taking a turn-off from the N125. It boasts some accommodation, a few restaurants on the promenade by the lagoon and a boat service that ferries you the short distance to the entrance of the attractive **Praia de Cabanas**.

A romantic twilight scene: the old port on the Rio Gilão

The cityscape here is defined by the church's clock tower and the former water tower. The latter, known as the **Torre de Tavira**, is home to a **camera obscura** today (►see box). The upper part of the Old Town boasts a Pousada hotel in an old monastery and the **Igreja de Santiago**, a richly decorated 17th-century church that's astonishingly large despite only having one nave.

TAKING A BREAK

The Praça da República – Tavira's central square near the river – is a great place to take a break.

🗺 206 A1 🚌 Rua dos Pelames; connections to Faro, Lisbon, Olhão, Vila Real de Santo António, etc.; www.eva-bus.com 🚉 Largo de Santo Amaro; connections to Faro, Lagos, Lisbon, Vila Real de Santo António, etc.; www.cp.pt

Posto de Turismo
✉ Praça da República 5 ☎ 281 322 511; www.cm-tavira.pt
🕐 Tue–Thu 9:30am–7pm, Fri–Mon 10am–1pm, 3pm–7pm

Núcleo Museológico Islâmico
✉ Praça da República ☎ 281 320 570; http://museumunicipaldetavira.tavira.pt
🕐 Summer: Tue–Sat 10am–12:30 & 3–6:30pm; rest of year: Tue–Sat 10am–12:30 & 2–5:30pm 💷 €2; €3 with the Palácio da Galeria

Igreja da Misericórdia
✉ Largo da Misericórdia 🕐 Tue–Sat 9am–12:30/1pm, 2–6pm 💷 Free

Palácio da Galeria/Museu Municipal
✉ Calçada da Galeria ☎ 281 320 540; http://museumunicipaldetavira.tavira.pt
🕐 Tue–Sat 9:30am–12:30 and 3pm–6:30pm in summer; Tue–Sat 9:30am–12:30 and 2pm–5:30pm during the rest of the year
💷 €2; €3 in combination with the Núcleo Museológico Islâmico

Igreja de Santa Maria do Castelo/Museu de Arte Sacra
✉ Calçada da Galeria 🕐 Mon–Sat 10am–1pm & 2–5/5:30pm 💷 €1.50

Igreja de Santiago
✉ Rua Don Paio Peres Correia 🕐 Mon–Fri 9:30am–noon 💷 Free

⭐8 Rio Guadiana

The Rio Guadiana is one of the major rivers on the Iberian Peninsula. Its source lies in the middle of southern Spain. Towards the end of its nearly 750km (470mi)-long journey to the Atlantic, the river marks out the border between Spain and Portugal. It's here that the Rio Guadiana meets the eastern Algarve.

The name *Guadiana* has Arabic origins, and was presumably derived from *Wadi Yanah* ("wadi" means "river"). The river was once a navigable waterway that stretched far inland. Ships used it to transport ore from the São Domingos mines and all kinds of agricultural goods. The Rio Guadiana lost its significance as a trading route long ago. Nevertheless, it still feeds such reservoirs as the Barragem de Alqueva in the Alentejo, and remains important for all the agricultural regions it passes through. It's also an attractive sight for tourists! You can get close to the Rio Guadiana at several places in the eastern Algarve, including in **Alcoutim** (► 72) and **Foz de Odeleite**, along with all the river promenade in **Vila Real de Santo António** (► 76), and to the south of the same city, where a narrow and extremely bumpy road runs parallel to the river on its way to the **estuary**.

Travelling down the River

Insider Tip
If you really want to discover the Rio Guadiana, book a **river cruise** in Vila Real de Santo António. Providers such as Riosul (► see box) offer full day tours (from around 10am to 5pm). Just so you know before you book, you'll be ferried around in groups. You should also be aware that the tours usually start with a drive (in jeeps) to the boarding point at **Foz de Odeleite**. Stops along the way are possible – you might be able to visit the salt producing area near **Castro Marim** or go to see craftspeople at work, for example. Before the boat trip gets underway, you'll be served a typical local lunch at a country estate (included in the price). Afterwards, you'll weigh anchor in **Foz de Odeleite** and head off along the river. It's 100m (330ft) wide in places and often looks muddy brown in colour. The current is bordered by shallow hills as the water loops its way through the landscape. You'll occasionally pass yachts moored in the middle of the water-way. Bushes crowd the

The Ponte Internacional do Guadiana, a cable-stayed bridge at the mouth of the river, links Portugal with Spain. It's a popular spot for photos on boat trips

The Cruzeiro no Guadiana, a day-long **Guadiana boat tour** from Riosultravel (tel. 281 510 200; www.riosultravel.com) costs upwards of €47 per person. They offer a pick-up service from your hotel – the price depends on how far you're staying from the starting point in Vila Real de Santo António. River tours are also offered by Transguadiana (tel. 281 512 997; www.transguadiana.com).

riverbanks, and oranges and mandarins grow in the small adjacent fields.

Towards the Bridge and the Estuary

The Rio Guadiana grows broader and broader the closer you get to the estuary and the modern highway bridge (built in the early 1990s). Just before the bridge, the water swells to around 300m (985ft) in width. Passing under the structure itself is an interesting experience – the traffic between Spain and Portugal whizzes over your heads.

On the right, you'll see the **Reserva Natural do Sapal** (► 78) nature reserve that's interspersed with wetlands and salt marshes. It's home to numerous varieties of bird. The twin fortresses on the hills at **Castro Marim** (► 74) rise up in the distance. From here, it's not far to **Vila Real de Santo António** (► 76).

TAKING A BREAK

Explore the area around the marina in Vila Real de Santo António (► 76) – you'll find some nice spots by the river and a few good places to eat.

✚ 206 C3

⑪ Alcoutim

A friendly, tranquil atmosphere surrounds this town on the Rio Guadiana (► 70). But don't be fooled by appearances – this wasn't always the case. The castle was once used to protect the river and fend off attacks from across the Spanish border.

Alcoutim's location on the Rio Guadiana played a decisive role in the town's development. The push and pull of the Atlantic tides were felt this far up stream, meaning that ships transporting goods were often forced to stop here and wait for more favourable conditions. As a result, a certain amount of infrastructure was built for shipping in the town and the fortress was constructed to monitor and defend the traffic on the river.

🎿 FLY OVER THE GUADIANA

A fun tourist attraction in Alcoutim lets you fly right across the Rio Guadiana (well, sort of!) A 700m (765yd)-long zipline suspended above the water shoots you across at speeds of up to 70–80km/h (45–50mph). Young people and older kids will love it. The operator, stationed across from Alcoutim on the Spanish side of the river, is called Limitezero (Avenida de Portugal, 21595 Sanlúcar de Guadiana, www.limitezero.com, Spanish mobile 0034 670 313 933). The whole exhilarating experience costs €17 per person. A ferry takes you over to Spain before you hurtle back to Portugal along the wire.

A Castle with a View

Once used by the Moors, the *Castelo Velho* (Old Castle) was abandoned as early as the 11th/12th century. The biggest draw for visitors today is the more recently built **castelo** dating from the late Middle Ages. Sitting high above the small village centre and the Rio Guadiana border river, it was adapted to deal with artillery attacks in the 17th century.

Today, the fortress is a true oasis of calm that's filled with greenery. It's also home to the incongruously styled **Núcleo Museológico de Arqueologia** (Archaeological Museum). *Insider Tip* The highlight has to be the wonderful views out over the river and across to Spain.

Beautiful Riverbanks

Take a stroll through Alcoutim to the main church (the 16th-century **Igreja Matriz**), the main square (the **Praça da República**) and the nicely appointed riverside zone. You can't get lost: everything's confined to a very small area indeed. Flower boxes and ceramic pots sit by the front doors, and the windows and door surrounds bring a bit of colour to the tranquil streets.

The views over the roofs of Alcoutim reach right across into neighbouring Spain

The restaurants around the Praça da República are a good place to settle down for a bite to eat in Alcoutim's cosy town centre.

🔢 206 C5

Posto de Turismo
✉ Rua 1° de Maio ☎ 281 546 179; www.cm-alcoutim.pt

Castelo (Núcleo Museológico de Arqueologia)
🕙 April–Sept, daily 9–7. Oct–Mar, daily 9:30–5:30 💶 €2.50

INSIDER INFO

- Alcoutim isn't just a nice destination – you can also explore a bit of the **Algarve's interior** on your way there. You'll get close to the Rio Guadiana (➤ 70) if you drive between Foz de Odeleite and Alcoutim, something you should do at least once on your outward or return journey. The trip along the country highways that pass via Odeleite on their way northwest from Vila Real de Santo António and Castro Marim also offer beautiful views of the **Barragem de Odeleite** reservoir, where you'll see a number of small islands peeking out of the clear, blue water.
- Alcoutim lies at the intersection of **two major long-distance hiking routes**. The 65km (40mi)-long GR15 runs here from Vila Real de Santo António in the south, and the Via Algarviana stretches all the way out to the Cabo de São Vicente (➤ 127), the Algarve's westernmost point.
- If you're driving to Alcoutim, you can easily extend your trip by making a **detour to the neighbouring Alentejo region**. The first worthwhile stop there is the village of Mértola with its fortress and church (➤ Tours, 182).

⑫ Castro Marim

The twin fortress on the hills of Castro Marim give you an idea of how important the town once was for controlling the nearby Rio Guadiana (▶ 70) and defending the region against Spain. Peace reigns here today, but it's still bustling thanks to the thriving salt economy in the surrounding countryside.

Castro Marim can be seen from far and wide, sticking up from the flat lands west of the nascent Rio Guadiana estuary and the wetlands and salt marshes nearby. The town's forts, spread across two hills, clearly give away its position. The Forte São Sebastião (17th c.) is not open to visitors, but the ramparts of the much older – and much more historically significant – **castelo** from the late-Middle Ages are just ready and waiting to be explored.

Salt plays an important role in the local economy

Fortifications already stood on this spot during the Moorish period. The current building was constructed by King Alfonso III in the 13th century.

Historic Seat of the Order of Christ

The castelo provides visitors with a fantastic opportunity to dive headfirst into the long history of the region. Although the fortress has suffered greatly over the centuries and now seems more like a patchwork of stone in places, the structure of the original Moorish fortifications – a castle within a castle – can still be seen today. It's also interesting to note that the fort served as the headquarters of the

---

SIGNS OF THE SALT INDUSTRY

The salt industry around Castro Marim – which uses the evaporation technique to create its wares – produces salt for a variety of purposes and markets. Inferior quality salt is sent to the fish canning industry in North Africa, for example, and machines are used in making salt for roads from industrial salt pans. The very best quality salt is *flor de sal* ("flower of salt"), a luxury that's prized by foodies and gourmet restaurants alike. It's costly and complicated to produce: it forms wafer-thin layers on the surface of the water which have to be skimmed off and dried. The resultant crunchy, crystalline flakes are sold in packets. The main salt harvest takes place in August and September. The salt marshes – which make up part of the surrounding Reserva Natural do Sapal (▶ 78) nature reserve – are visited by a wide variety of birds, including pink-feathered flamingos.

Military Order of Christ (the successors to the Knights Templar) for a time in the 14th century. A museum area with some historical artefacts has been added to the complex. The view from the castle walls stretches out over the Forte São Sebastião, the Rio Guadiana, the motorway bridge across the water, and the surrounding salt works.

The Church and the Lower Village
The domed **Igreja Matriz** – the main church that dates from the 18th/19th century and stands below the castelo – is a striking historical monument. The rest of the modest lower part of the village largely consists of a few streets and alleyways around the Rua de São Sebastião, the Rua José Alves Moreira and the Rua de São Gonçalo de Lagos.

TAKING A BREAK
You'll find some places to eat along the Rua de São Sebastião and the Rua José Alves Moreira in the lower part of the village..

The white village contrasts with the old fortress of the Knights of Christ

🞢 206 C2

Posto de Turismo
✉ Rua José Alves Moreira 2–4 ☎ 281 531 232; www.cm-castromarim.pt

Castelo
🕐 May–Sept, daily 9–7; Oct–Apr, daily 9–5 🎟 €1.10

⑬ Vila Real de Santo António

Founded in the 18th century, this city owes its charm to its location by the Rio Guadiana (➤ 70) and its bustling centre, which stretches out in a chessboard pattern of ruler-straight streets around the Praça Marquês de Pombal.

Vila Real de Santo António was founded in 1774 thanks to a programme of precise planning efforts and some clear political and economic objectives. The city was created first and foremost to increase State control in the region. The powers that be wanted to keep as close an eye as possible on the flow of goods travelling along the Rio Guadiana and put a stop to smuggling. What's more, they wanted to place the fishing industry in nearby Monte Gordo (➤ 79) under royal supervision – a move which would later bring the vital fish canning industry to the city. Vila Real de Santo António was also born from a need to display a stronger presence along the Rio Guadiana. This was done to ward off Spain – their neighbours across the river – who had often caused problems in the past.

A Lisbon-style Chessboard Layout

The new city of Vila Real de Santo António was built following a pattern that had proved successful when the lower part of Lisbon was reconstructed after the mighty earthquake of 1755. This chessboard layout eschewed all the traditional winding curves and labyrinthine alleyways, replacing them instead with functional, unfussy architecture, straight roads and a main square. This square was named after Sebastião José de Carvalho e Melo, better known as the Marquês de Pombal (1699–1782), a man whose career as a statesman gathered steam during the reign of King José I and who was instrumental in the creation of Vila Real de Santo António itself.

The obelisk stands in memory of the people who organised the rebuilding of Vila Real de Santo António from 1774

An Obelisk of Power

The obelisk in the centre of the **Praça Marquês de Pombal** stands as a symbol of the King's and the Marquis (Marquês) of Pombal's power. The square is lined with two 18th-century buildings – the Town Hall and the **main church**, the Igreja Matriz de Nossa Senhora da Encarnação. The church's statue of the Virgin Mary (the *Nossa*

The tranquil marina in the morning sun

Senhora da Encarnação) is the work of the sculptor Joaquim Machado de Castro. The electric candles inside the church are a piece of 21st-century technology. This isn't the first time that Vila Real de Santo António has embraced modern illumination – in the late 1800s, it became the first city in the Algarve to have gas lighting.

An Atmospheric Backdrop

The vibrant cafés and restaurants around the Praça Marquês de Pombal are pulsating with life. Go and immerse yourself in the constant hustle and bustle. The square occasionally provides an excellent backdrop for open-air concerts and markets. You can also wander away from the square along the streets of the pedestrian zone, where shopping is the main attraction (► 85).

Insider Tip

The River Promenade

The Praça Marquês de Pombal is no more than a few minutes' walk from the nicely appointed **promenade** on the **Rio Guadiana** that boasts benches, palm trees, a river harbour and various restaurants. The Rio Guadiana flows into Atlantic just a few miles further on.

TAKING A BREAK

There's no shortage of open-air terraces around the Praça Marquês de Pombal! Sit down for a bite to eat if you want the best views for a spot of people-watching.

➕ 206 C2 ℹ️ www.cm-vrsa.pt 🚌 Avenida da República; connections to Alcoutim, Castro Marim, Faro, Monte Gordo, etc.; www.eva-bus.com 🚆 Largo da Estação; trains to Faro and Lagos, etc.; www.cp.pt

INSIDER INFO

The municipal **Centro Cultural Antonio Aleixo** in the Rua Teófilo Braga sometimes acts as a venue for exhibitions and smaller events.

At Your Leisure

Dreamy: the Praia de Monte Verde

⑭ Reserva Natural do Sapal
This small nature reserve extends over an area of around 2,100 hectares (5,190 acres) near **Castro Marim** (➤ 74) and **Vila Real de Santo António** (➤ 76) and meets

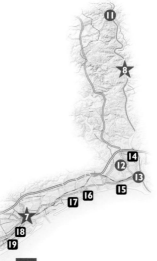

the **Rio Guadiana** (➤ 70) in the east. *Sapal* means "wetland" – a natural feature that, along with the salt marshes, covers a large part of the surrounding landscape. Although not entirely unspoilt (note the settlements and the signs of the salt industry), the area is a major ecological sanctuary that provides a habitat for over **150 species of bird, including flamingos, white storks and black-winged stilts.** You'll also have a good chance of spotting flamingos in the **salt marshes** around Castro Marim. Unless otherwise stated, anyone's free to use the surfaced dirt tracks that run past the wetlands.

Insider Tip

The **Nature Park Visitor Centre** (Centro de Interpretação) can be seen from the motorway bridge over the Rio Guadiana. To reach it, take the turn-off from the country highway between Castro Marim and Odeleite as you draw level with São Francisco. An interesting **round walk** starts at the car park.

FUN AT THE BEACH

Summer sun, sea & sand: some further beaches that are worth a visit to the east of Manta Rota on the route to Monte Gordo (➤ 79) include the **Praia do Cabeço**, the **Praia de Monte Verde** and the **Praia de Alagoa**. If you head east from Monte Gordo towards the Rio Guadiana estuary (➤ 70), you'll pass several more wide, sandy beaches. They are bordered with dunes and are somewhat more secluded. The **Praia de Santo António** is also good *Insider Tip* for 👪 families with children – kids can have a lot of fun there collecting shells.

It leads to a hill with beautiful views over the salt marshes and the Rio Guadiana.

✚ 206 C2

🄸 Monte Gordo

It's a little odd that this town has *monte* ("mountain") in its name – you won't see any real hills for miles around. A major attraction here is the long, wide **sandy beach**, part of which is still used by fishermen. Monte Gordo doesn't have a harbour, so the fishermen work together to drag their **fishing boats** up on the sand. These vessels, decorated with colourful flags, offer some great photo opportunities.

It's an inconvenient truth that the rise of tourism in the 1960s led to the construction of the concrete high-rises that blight this seaside resort. Despite this, the area's natural beauty remains in tact, both on the beach and in the **pine forests** that can be seen to the west and east of Monte Gordo itself. The visitors who come to the holiday resort are an international crowd – it's particularly popular with the Dutch. The beach promenade itself is very nice. If you want to gamble away your holiday budget, head to the casino.

A view of the lagoon by Cacela Velha

✚ 206 C1 🚍 connections to Faro, Luz de Tavira, Olhão, Tavira and Vila Real de Santo António, etc.; www.eva-bus.com

Posto de Turismo
✉ Avenida Infante D. Henrique (behind the beach) ☎ 281 544 495; www.cm-vrsa.pt
🕐 Tue–Thu 9:30–7, Fri–Mon 9:30–1, 2–5:30

🄼 Manta Rota

Summer and winter are as different as night and day here: there's a party atmosphere in summer and it's dead quiet in winter. The long, wide **sandy beach** bordered by dunes and gigantic car parks is the resort's extremely popular focal point. Walkways lead down to the sand over the dunes.

Unlike the concrete jungle at Monte Gordo, Manta Rota is far more low-rise and much more pleasant to look at. Hibiscus shrubs dominate the streetscape. The beach right next door is called the Praia da Lota.

✚ 206 B1

🄽 Cacela Velha

This small, picturesque village lies beyond the N125, about halfway between Tavira and Monte Gordo. It's an historically protected settlement that sits high above the eastern offshoots of the

Boat trips head out from Tavira into the lagoon landscape

lagoon-filled **Parque Natural da Ria Formosa** (➤ 108). It's best to park on the edge of the village and stroll through the alleyways up to the viewing point by the church. Let the houses' pretty chimneys and bright blue-and-yellow painted facades work their photogenic magic on you as you make your way up on foot.

Insider Tip

A square and a street are named in memory of two poets from the Moorish era – Ibn Darraj Al Qastalli and Abû Al Abdarî. An extensive lagoon landscape stretches out beneath the village itself. As you look out over the vista, your eye will be drawn time and again to the bizarre prickly pear cacti and the small fields scattered all around. The small fortress isn't open to visitors, but you can take a stroll through the **cemetery** at the edge of the village. The multi-storey graves complete with pull-out compartments, artificial flowers, candlesticks and photos of the deceased are typical of a Portuguese burial ground. The grander tombs show off their coffins through glass panels, which can be a little creepy. Visitors aren't allowed to film or take pictures.
✠ 206 B1

18 Santa Luzia

This nice, unspoilt village south-west of Tavira sits opposite the **Ilha de Tavira** (➤ below). Waterways separate the settlement from the elongated island. Santa Luzia is a **centre of octopus fishing**, something you'll see reflected in the restaurants' menus. The numerous small fishing boats are particularly photogenic in the evening, but it's worth taking a stroll along the **promenade** at any time of day. During the holiday season, boat shuttle services ferry people over to the **Praia da Terra Estreita**, a beach on the Ilha de Tavira.
✠ 205 F2

19 Ilha de Tavira

The Ilha de Tavira – a flat, elongated island – belongs to the **Parque Natural da Ria Formosa** (➤ 108) and thrills visitors with its seemingly unending expanses of beach. Boat shuttles regularly run there from **Tavira** (➤ 66), ferrying visitors to the island from the Quatro Águas landing point. There are also some boats that'll take you there from the old Mercado da Ribeira market halls nearer Tavira's city centre in summer. The boats head for the far northeast of the island, where big restaurants and a summer camp-site have been set up to deal with the stream of visitors. The further you go away from these tourist facilities, the more isolated and authentic the beach becomes. If you're walking across the sand with children in tow, it's a great place to indulge in a spot of shell collecting.

You can also reach the middle of the Ilha de Tavira by traversing a causeway (approx. 1km/0.6mi long) to the southwest of **Santa Luzia** (➤ 80), a village famous for its octopus fishing. You can either make the journey across by foot or aboard a quaint miniature railway. There's a small area with some refreshment stops behind the train's final station. The complex was originally built in the mid-19th century as a result of tuna fishing.

Your destination on the island sits just beyond the dunes. Head for the **Praia do Barril**, a wonderful sandy beach that stretches to the left and right as far as the eye can see. The curious **Cemitério das Âncoras** ("Anchor Cemetery") lies in the dunes behind the beach.

This is a site where a host of fishing boat anchors have found

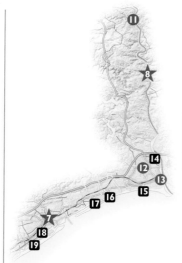

their final resting place in the sand. Numbering in the triple digits, they're one of the strangest sights you'll see in the Algarve. They seem to have been left there as a monument to the end of tuna fishing in the region. The Praia do Barril also offers visitors the chance to try out a variety of water sports in the holiday season.

✚ 205 F2

Insider Tip

The Parque Natural da Ria Formosa is particularly colourful in spring

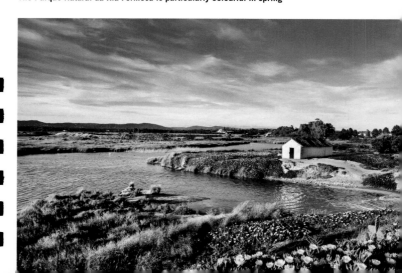

Where to...
Stay

Prices
for a double room per night in the high season
€ under 90 euros   €€ 90–150 euros   €€€ over 150 euros

CABANAS DE TAVIRA

Pedras da Rainha €–€€
You can choose from a selection of studios and houses to rent in this large complex that's located a short way away from the heart of Cabanas de Tavira. The site, which also includes a number of private holiday homes, is a great place for self-caterers. The units are equipped for two to ten people and are well-suited to 👪 families with children. It's just ten minutes' walk to the restaurant area on the promenade, from where some boats also ferry passengers over to the Praia de Cabanas. Pedras da Rainha also boasts some large lawns, an open-air pool, several tennis courts and a restaurant. The prices are attractive, especially during the off-season. You'll find MegaSport (www.megasport.pt), a seasonal bike-hire shop, right by the entrance to the complex itself.
🔲 206 B1
✉ On your right as you approach Cabanas de Tavira from the N125
☎ 281 380 680; http://pedrasdarainha.com

CASTRO MARIM

Quinta da Fornalha €–€€
Insider Tip
The Quinta da Fornalha eco-avoid is perfect if you want to escape a typical beach vacation and experience a touch of country living instead. It's surrounded by fig plantations. Such products as pickled figs and fig chutney are on sale in the farm shop. They rent out studios and cottages for self-caterers (a total of six units with different facilities).
🔲 206 C2 ✉ A few kilometers southwest of Castro Marim on the road that leads via São Bartolomeu on its way to the N125 (the turn-off is signposted)
☎ 281 541 733; www.quinta-da-fornalha.com
🕐 Only rented by the week from mid-July–end Aug.

MONTE GORDO

Vasco da Gama €€–€€€
We know what you're going to say… this is one of those hotel blocks that hasn't exactly helped to beautify Monte Gordo. But bear with us, there's a big bonus in store: it's right next to the wide sandy beach (with no road in between). It also has a pool. Prices depend on the view from your room. Apartments are also available to rent.
🔲 206 C1
✉ Avenida Infante D. Henrique
☎ 281 510 900; www.vascodagamahotel.com

SANTA LUZIA

Pedras d'el Rei €–€€
This sprawling complex offers guests a choice of studios, apartments and holiday homes that are suitable for two to eight people. It's also a good place for 👪 families with kids. The miniature railway that heads over the causeway towards the Praia da Barril on the Ilha de Tavira (▶ 80) is only a short walk away. The train is free for anyone staying at the *Insider Tip*

hotel. If you fancy a change, you can easily walk over to the island instead. The resort boasts some large lawns and an outdoor pool. There's also a restaurant: the Restaurante Vale d'el Rei (➤ 84).

🔤 205 F2
✉ Southwest of Santa Luzia
☎ 281 380 600; http://pedrasdelrei.com

TAVIRA

Almargem Lusitano €–€€
An ideal place for fans of country house tourism. It's a long way from Tavira, so ask for the exact directions when making your booking – it'll save you a lot of time searching when you arrive! They have ten rooms in total, and the prices are graded according to the facilities they offer. It's simple, solid and clean inside, and there's a tasteful outdoor area. The small pool is perfect for a cooling dip.

🔤 206 A1   ✉ Sítio do Almargem
☎ 281 323 386; www.almargemlusitano.com

Vila Galé Albacora €€€
If you'd enjoy staying in an isolated spot in the middle of nature, then this is the place for you. The hotel is located around 4km (2.5mi) east of Tavira in the Parque Natural da Ria Formosa (➤ 108) and boasts a large pool area and a boat shuttle service to the Ilha de Tavira (➤ 80). It's interesting to note that the low-rise complex stands on the site of a former tuna processing plant – you can still see some signs of this history today.

🔤 206 A1   ✉ Quatro Águas
☎ 281 380 800; www.vilagale.com
🕐 closed in Winter

Vila Galé Tavira €€€
A second hotel from the tried-and-tested Vila Galé hotel chain. This four-star residence near the centre of Tavira has an impressively big foyer, but its real heart is the outdoor pool that's surrounded by three storeys of rooms. Guests have a small spa and fitness area and a large restaurant zone at their disposal. It can be worth staying here in the off-season – the prices you'll pay will be significantly lower.

Insider Tip

🔤 206 A1   ✉ Rua 4 de Outubro
☎ 281 329 900; www.vilagale.com

Where to...
Eat and Drink

Prices
for a three-course set menu without drinks or service
€ under 20 euros   €€ 20–35 euros   €€€ over 35 euros

CACELA VELHA

Casa Velha €–€€
Head slightly upwards past the lemon trees to this welcoming, long-established village restaurant and find yourself a seat out in the large interior courtyard. The selection of typical, tasty homemade cooking on offer ranges from omelettes and salad to octopus rice and grilled fish. The cuisine is simple but delicious and proves very popular with the local population.

🔤 206 B1
✉ At the entrance to the village (coming from the car park)
☎ 281 952 297
🕐 Tue–Sun noon–3pm & 7–10pm

Eastern Algarve

PRAIA DO CABEÇO

Sem Espinhas €€

The name of this beach restaurant means "without bones", but they obviously can't guarantee that the fish they serve will be entirely free of spiny surprises! There's also a selection of meat dishes and salads on offer. The beachside location is a real plus. It stands on the same site as its predecessor, a popular beach shack that was set up in the 1970s.

🚩 206 C1
✉ Praia do Cabeço, Castro Marim
☎ 281 956 026; www.semespinhas.net
🕐 Open seasonally, daily 10am–7pm

SANTA LUZIA

Casa do Polvo €

As you might expect, everything at the Casa do Polvo (which means "House of Octopus" in Portuguese) is geared towards the local speciality from Santa Luzia. A meal here is a real treat for octopus fans. The eatery is even rated highly by locals (a very good sign indeed!) You'll find the restaurant quite easily if you head out along the road that runs parallel to the lagoon.

🚩 206 A1
✉ Avenida Engenheiro Duarte Pacheco 8
☎ 281 328 527
🕐 Wed–Mon noon–3pm & 6:30–10pm

Vale d'el Rei €€–€€€

This restaurant is part of the Pedras d'el Rei (►82) studio, apartment and holiday house complex that lies a short way to the southwest of Santa Luzia. Depending on the weather, you can take refuge in the cool interior or sit out on the forecourt with its terrace overlooking the lawns and the pool. The regional cuisine is excellent – they serve octopus dishes and a range of other local delicacies.

🚩 206 A1 ✉ Pedras d'el Rei, Santa Luzia
☎ 281 380 600, http://pedrasdelrei.com
🕐 Daily 12:30–3pm and 6:30–10:30pm

TAVIRA

A Ver Tavira €€

This restaurant boasts a wonderful location overlooking Tavira. It sits near the castle and the church of Santa Maria do Castelo. The view from the terrace is its biggest selling point and attracts a great many guests. It's hard to get excited about the food, which is solid and reliable.

🚩 206 A1 ✉ Calçada da Galeria 13
☎ 281 381 363 🕐 11am–midnight
(sometimes closed in winter)

Bica €–€€

This eatery has a number of things going for it: a warm atmosphere, a selection of delicious fish and seafood dishes (e.g. tuna, rice dishes, shrimps in garlic sauce), and a handful of tables in the narrow street in front of a façade that's covered in azulejos. They also serve meals cooked in a *cataplana* (►34). The lamb chops are a good alternative if you'd prefer to eat some meat.

🚩 206 A1
✉ Rua Almirante Cândido Reis 24–28
☎ 281 323 843 🕐 noon–2:30pm, 7pm–10pm

Pousada Convento da Graça €€€

This Pousada hotel is steeped in stylish ambience. You can either stay in one of the 36 rooms or enjoy an excellent meal at the restaurant. The building it's housed in – the Convento da Graça up on the hill in Tavira's Old Town – originally served as an Augustinian monastery (from the 16th/17th century). Alms, bread and soup were once given to the needy here. The kitchen is much more sophisticated today, and predominantly serves southern Portuguese cuisine along with a wide selection of wines.

🚩 206 A1
✉ Rua Dom Paio Peres Correia
☎ 210 407 680; www.pestana.com
🕐 Daily 12:30–3pm and 7:30–10pm

VILA REAL DE SANTO ANTÓNIO

Sem Espinhas €€

The Sem Espinhas, a restaurant with a terrace, belongs to the same small chain of eateries as the beach restaurant with a matching name on the Praia do Cabeço (►84). It sits in a central location beside the road that runs along the river. If you fancy an after-dinner stroll, simply cross the street and you'll find yourself on the beautiful Rio Guadiana promenade. The restaurant provides attentive service and has a sophisticated – but not overly elitist – ambience. The menu includes a nice range of fish, seafood and meat dishes. There's also a good selection of wines.

🏛 206 C2 ✉ Avenida da República 51
☎ 281 544 605; www.semespinhas.net
🕐 Daily 11am–10:30pm

Where to...
Shop

Vila Real de Santo António is a very popular place to shop. The city centre boasts rows and rows of stores. Lots of Spanish people cross the border for some retail therapy as things tend to be cheaper here. The Praça Marquês de Pombal is the best place to start. You'll find a downright staggering array of large and small towels, tea towels, tablecloths and kitchen aprons wherever you go.

THE ROOSTER OF BARCELOS

Prints of the Rooster of Barcelos make a lovely souvenir, but you can't leave the Algarve without some idea of what the legend is all about... Once upon a time in the Middle Ages, a pilgrim heading through northern Portugal stopped off in Barcelos on his way to the tomb of St James in the Spanish town of Santiago de Compostela. Before he knew it, he had been accused of committing a crime and was sentenced to death by hanging. As his final wish, he asked to see the judge one last time. He was duly brought to the lawman, who was busy eating a rooster. "If I am innocent, that rooster will crow", declared the pilgrim, much to everyone's amusement. But at that very moment, the rooster let forth a cry... and the innocent man was set free.

CRAFTS AND SALT

Tavira is also good for a spot of window shopping, particularly around the Rua Dr. José Pires Padinha near the river and on the bustling Rua da Liberdade. The Associação de Artes e Sabores, an association dedicated to all kinds of crafts and culinary products, has its headquarters in Tavira. Their shop, the **Casa do Artesão** at Calçada da Galeria 11 (up on the hill in the Old Town), sells cork goods, decorative tiles, bags, costume jewellery, sweets, fig brandy, homemade liqueurs, etc. You can stock up on salt – including the highly sought-after *flor de sal* ("flower of salt") – in **Castro Marim**.

Insider Tip

MARKETS

Flea and junk markets *(feiras de velharias)* are very popular. They all take place at regular venues and times: by the Mercado Municipal in Tavira on the 1st and 5th Saturday of the month; by the Posto de Turismo in Monte Gordo on the 4th Saturday of the month; and on the Praça Marquês de Pombal in Vila Real de Santo António on the 2nd Saturday of the month. **Markets** *(mercados)* are held e.g. in

Eastern Algarve

Castro Marim on the 2nd Saturday; on the Rua Almirante Cândido dos Reis (at the football field) in Tavira on the 3rd Saturday; and on the Praça Marquês de Pombal in Vila Real de Santa António on the 1st Sunday of the month.

Where to…
Go Out

Tavira is both the cultural centre and the nightlife hub of the eastern Algarve. It boasts a wide selection of bars and places to go out (some with live music). Beach resorts like Monte Gordo also get pretty lively at night during the holiday season. Head to tourist offices to get the free "Algarve Guia/Guide". Published every month, it tells you all about festivals, events, exhibitions, sports fixtures, etc.

CINEMAS & CONCERTS

You can go to the movies at the **Tavira Gran-Plaza** (www.tavira granplaza.com) shopping centre and at the Cine Teatro Antonio Pinheiro (Rua Guilherme Gomes Fernandes; www.cine clube-tavira. com). Concerts are sometimes held in the **Igreja da Misericórdia**.

FADO

Recommended: the **Fado com História** cultural association organises short fado concerts in a small room by the Igreja da Misericórdia from Monday to Saturday. The music is performed by a singer with guitar accompaniment. (Rua Damião Augusto de Brito Vasconcelos 4; for dates, visit http://fado comhistoria.wix. com/fado; tel. 968 774 613, approx. 20 mins, €5).

FUN ON THE WATER

Boat tours through the lagoon-filled landscape of the Parque Natural da Ria Formosa are just one of the leisure activities that are ideal for 👫families with kids. Sequa Tours (tel. 960 170 789; www.sequa tours.com) set off from Tavira. They also run bird-watching trips. The standard lagoon tour lasting around an hour costs €12 per person. A more extended two-hour tour is €35. If you want an adrenaline rush, take a **zipline** in Alcoutim over the Rio Guadiana, the Spanish-Portuguese border river (www.limitezero.com, ➤ 70). You can also take **kite surfing** lessons at Cabanas de Tavira (Kitesurf Eolis, Av. Ria Formosa 8, Centro Comercial, Loja 34, tel. 962 337 285; www.kitesurfeolis.com).

HIKING, BIKING & GOLFING

You can go for a walk along parts of the Via Algarviana (www.via-algarviana.com), the long-distance hiking route that starts in Alcoutim and ends at the Cabo de São Vicente (➤ 127) in the west. A more recent addition is the GR15 distance hiking path, which stretches out along a 65km (40mi) route between Alcoutim and Vila Real de Santo António. The pine forests around Monte Gordo are well suited to jogging and shorter walks. It's also worth taking a stroll through the lagoon landscape of the Ria Formosa by Cabanas (to the east of Tavira). **Cyclists** will enjoy trying out sections of the Ecovia (➤ 179), the long-distance track that runs near the coast. Note that parts of the route head along a main road, however. You can also go **golfing** near Castro Marim (www.castromarimresort.com) and Vila Nova de Cacela (at the Quinta de Cima and Quinta da Ria resorts; www.quintadaria.com), for example.

Faro & Central Algarve

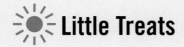 **Little Treats**

Fisherman's Friend

You'll feel like a fisherman if you stop for refreshments in the village of Culatra on the **Ilha da Culatra** (➤ 98) and stroll through the island's traffic-free streets.

Amazing Azulejos

Head to the Ermida de Nossa Senhora da Conceição in **Loulé** (➤ 113) to marvel at the magnificent decorative tiles.

I Got Rhythm

The **O Farol** bar (➤ 108) near the lagoon in **Fuseta** sometimes has live music.

Getting Your Bearings

The central Algarve is a melting pot of contrasting natural landscapes. It's where the Atlantic meets the hilly hinterland and where long, sandy beaches encounter the labyrinth of canals and islands in the Parque Natural da Ria Formosa. In the centre of the region lies Faro, the capital of the Algarve and the point of arrival for countless holidaymakers. With its crystal clear light, glittering nightlife, fantastic beaches and fabulous markets, the central Algarve has a wealth of diverse experiences to offer.

The contrasts of the central Algarve begin in **Faro**, where the Old Town with its cathedral and historic walls sits right next to the picturesque marina. Head just outside the city to enjoy views out over parts of the **Parque Natural da Ria Formosa**, a natural park that stretches across to the eastern Algarve. It's dominated by shellfish farming, waterways and islands. The **Ilha da Culatra**, a beautiful island with a village atmosphere that

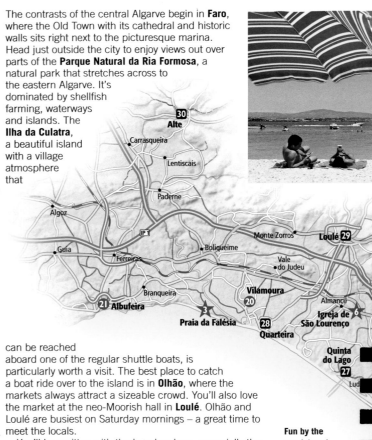

can be reached
aboard one of the regular shuttle boats, is particularly worth a visit. The best place to catch a boat ride over to the island is in **Olhão**, where the markets always attract a sizeable crowd. You'll also love the market at the neo-Moorish hall in **Loulé**. Olhão and Loulé are busiest on Saturday mornings – a great time to meet the locals.

You'll be smitten with the beaches here, especially the **Praia da Falésia** in **Albufeira** with its particularly high concentration of hotels. If you want to party the night away, go to Albufeira and Faro. You're also guaranteed to find something going on at night if you head to **Vilamoura**

Fun by the sea (above) and an evening stroll through Olhão (top right)

Getting Your Bearings

TOP 10

Don't Miss

At Your Leisure

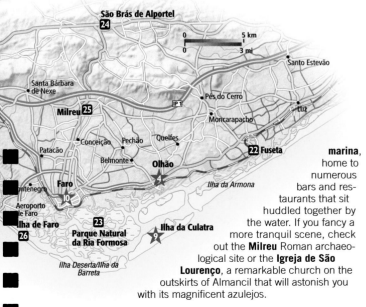

marina, home to numerous bars and restaurants that sit huddled together by the water. If you fancy a more tranquil scene, check out the **Milreu** Roman archaeological site or the **Igreja de São Lourenço**, a remarkable church on the outskirts of Almancil that will astonish you with its magnificent azulejos.

Three Perfect Days

This itinerary is a great way to see all of the most interesting destinations in the central Algarve in just three days without ever feeling rushed off your feet – it's important to enjoy the cuisine and the southern pace of life while you're here, after all! You'll need a (rental) car for the tour. When planning your trip, keep an eye on the opening hours of the markets and attractions.

Day One

Morning
Give yourself enough time to experience ⭐ **Faro** (➤ 100, harbour, image above) in the morning. Its streets, cathedral and the local museum in the former convent of Nossa Senhora da Assunção are all waiting to be discovered inside the historic city walls. Head outside the fortifications and take a stroll along the marina. You could also pay a visit to the eerie Bone Chapel (➤ 102) at the **Igreja do Carmo** before finding somewhere for lunch back in Faro.

Afternoon
It's now time to head to the beach! Drive a good distance northwest from Faro to the ⭐ **Praia da Falésia** (➤ 92, image below right), a particularly beautiful, cliff-lined stretch of sand that's several kilometres long. Various accessways lead down to the beach.

Evening
Keep the evening free to explore ⑳ **Vilamoura** (➤ 103) and the bustling atmosphere around the marina. It almost seems like there are as many bars and restaurants here as grains of sand on the beach next door!

Day Two

Morning
Start your day in ⭐ **Olhão** (➤ 94) and experience its true highlight – a stroll around the market. Afterwards, take the boat over to the ⭐ **Ilha da Culatra** (➤ 98). The crossing, which takes around 30 mins, lets you get

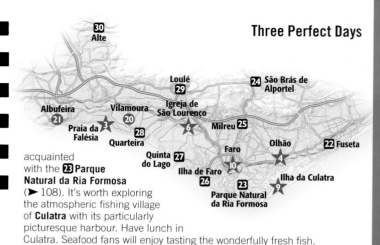

acquainted with the **23 Parque Natural da Ria Formosa** (➤ 108). It's worth exploring the atmospheric fishing village of **Culatra** with its particularly picturesque harbour. Have lunch in Culatra. Seafood fans will enjoy tasting the wonderfully fresh fish.

Afternoon
Spend some time on the beach behind **Culatra** before grabbing some refreshments in the village and clambering aboard the boat that'll take you back to **Olhão**.

Evening
22 Fuseta (➤ 106) is your destination for the evening. It's a nice little place with a few spots for dinner.

Day Three

Morning
Kick off your day by taking a short cultural trip inland to the Roman ruins of **25 Milreu** (➤ 110). They're not far from the village of Estoi. Afterwards, drive further out to the small city of **29 Loulé** (➤ 112) to have a walk around the market and eat a spot of lunch.

Afternoon/Evening
Before leaving Loulé, you might like to check out the small castle and the magnificent azulejos in the **Ermida de Nossa Senhora da Conceição** (➤ 112). If you're interested in azulejos, you could also visit the ★ **Igreja de São Lourenço** (➤ 96) near Almancil.

Even if it's getting late, the coastal city of **21 Albufeira** (➤ 104) has some nice areas to stroll around and stop for a bite to eat.

⭐❸ Praia da Falésia

Take a sandy beach, add some rust-brown cliffs and throw in a dash of the Atlantic. You'll be left with the Praia da Falésia – the longest beach in the Albufeira region and one of the most beautiful stretches of coast in the Algarve. If you're not yet sure why the Algarve is so popular with people from all over the world, one visit here will banish all doubt from your mind.

The eastern part of the Albufeira holiday resort is blessed with a seriously picture-perfect coastline. The Praia da Falésia stretches as far as the eye can see, and you can just make out Vilamoura marina (➤ 103) in the background. Steep cliffs rise up behind the beach, looking for all the world like they're a **backdrop from a Western**. These ragged rocks have been sculpted by nature to form mighty walls, towers, blocks and peaks.

Contrasting Shades
The walls of these cliffs rise up to around 30m (100ft) in height, and sometimes even a little higher. The rocks' dominant hue is rust red, but you'll also see ochre, browns and lighter tones mixed in here and there. And when the sun lends the sea a turquoise hue that any Caribbean island would be proud of, the colour contrasts are absolutely stunning.

Separated by Walls of Rock
At the top of the steep cliffs you'll see pine trees swaying in the wind, meadows filled with ice plants, and trails that often lead to good **vantage points**. It's also where you'll spot some wonderful **hotel complexes**, such as the Sheraton Algarve (➤ 114) and the neighbouring Pine Cliffs Resort (➤ 114). People with quite a lot of spare change use these hotels as a base. You'll come across lots of **paths running down to the beach**. It's not possible to reach the sand everywhere you go, however – in some places, the rock faces of the Praia da Falésia are too formidable to cross. That's also the reason why you won't find such facilities as beachside bars and deckchair rentals running the whole length of the beach. 🚸 Families with kids love

The edge of the cliffs sometimes collapse – this pine tree is clinging on for dear life

The shimmering red cliffs behind the Praia de Falésia are a characteristic sight in this part of the Algarve

coming here thanks to the broad expanses of sand and the shallow slope leading down into the water. People also enjoy walking along the long stretches of immaculately clean shore. If you're feeling less energetic, just lie back and enjoy the views of the impressive landscape all around you.

TAKING A BREAK

If you're planning a long walk along the Praia da Falésia towards Vilamoura, you'll find some places to stop for refreshments before you reach the marina itself.

➕ 201 E2

INSIDER INFO

- The colours of the cliff walls behind the Praia da Falésia look particularly impressive in the **morning and evening light**. Make sure to come at these times if you want to get some great photos.
- If you go for a walk along the cliff-top paths, make sure you **don't venture too close to the edge!** The cliffs can be fragile in places. And don't lie too near the bottom of the cliffs walls, either: it's not unknown for little bits of rock to break off and fall on unsuspecting sunbathers below.
- It's also worth **paying attention to the tide times**. If you spot a tide table, buy it. The higher the tide comes, the less beach area is left. When the sea level drops, the sand nearer the water is more solid and much easier to walk on.
- You'll find a number of other **extremely popular beaches** if you explore the area between the Praia da Falésia and the city of Albufeira to the west. They include the Praia de Santa Eulália, the Praia da Oura and the Praia de Maria Luisa.

Insider Tip

☆4 Olhão

You'd be hard pressed to find a bigger or better selection of fresh produce than you'll see on offer at the market halls in Olhão. One of the two large halls is dedicated to fish and seafood. This part of the harbour town has a fascinating, authentic atmosphere.

Visitors here will be astonished by the sights… and the smells! The **fish and seafood department** at Olhão market isn't the best place for people with a sensitive nose. The beautifully presented stalls offer a sensational selection, ranging from sardines and razor clams to squid, swordfish and tuna. Depending on the day's catch, you might also see

Insider Tip rays and small sharks on sale. It's a great (free!) way to learn about what lives in the Atlantic, what the fishermen are look-ing for, and what ends up on the tables of local restaurants. If you're staying in a self-catering studio or apartment, you definitely shouldn't miss the opportunity to come shopping at the market. If you'd like more than just fish, the second hall offers a selection of meat, fruit and vegetables.

Tightly packed: jostle with the locals in the fish hall (above) and join the crowds around the stands outside at the weekend (right)

Boats and an Open-air Market

The second market hall *(Mercados Municipais)* was built between 1912–1916 in an architectural style that was typical for the age. Apart from a new roof, the original structure remains intact. The halls border the lively Avenida 5 de Outubro on one side, and the promenade on the other. The latter offers views out over the watery landscape of the Parque Natural da Ria Formosa (➤ 108). A constant stream

INSIDER INFO

- Olhão is **pretty quiet on Mondays** – it's better to come another day.
- Held in August, the *Festival do Marisco* (Festival of Seafood) is a highlight of Olhão's social calendar. Attendees have plenty of chances to try out some delicious delicacies. The exact dates (around the middle of the month) and the programme of events can be found on the Festival do Marisco's Facebook page.
- Parts of the **fishing harbour** in Olhão aren't open to the public. Nevertheless, it's still a good place to take photos of the flocks of gulls and the fleet of fishing boats you'll spy here.
- If you fancy an interesting **walk** (➤ 186), stride out along the educational nature trail that runs through the characteristic wetlands of the **Parque Natural da Ria Formosa**.
- Shuttle boats set off from Olhão, travel through the Parque Natural da Ria Formosa and land at the **Ilha da Culatra** (➤ 98), the Ilha da Armona and the Ilha Deserta. Whatever you do, don't miss a chance to visit these **islands in the natural park**.

of **boats** sail past on their way to the major fishing harbour nearby. Try to come to Olhão on a **Saturday morning**. That's when there's a hive of activity around the market halls and

at the **open-air market** outside. Farmers, rural women and other small producers from the region come to sell their freshly harvested fruit and vegetables. Stalls also sell fashion jewellery, bags, sunglasses and tables stacked with a ragbag of clothes.

Another attraction in the centre of town is the **Igreja Matriz de Nossa Senhora do Rosário**, a Baroque church from the 17th/18th century. The faithful take votive offerings to the adjoining Aflitos chapel.

TAKING A BREAK

The space between the two market halls is a good place to settle down for a snack and a drink. You could also do a spot of people-watching while you take a breather.

✚ 205 D1 🚌 Rua General Humberto Delgado; connections to Faro, Fuseta, Lisbon, Monte Gordo, Tavira, Vila Real de Santo António, etc.; www.eva-bus.com

Posto de Turismo
✉ Largo Sebastião Martins Mestre 6 A ☎ 289 713 936; www.cm-olhao.pt

Market halls (Mercados Municipais)
✉ Avenida 5 de Outobro 🕐 Mon–Sat 7am–1pm

⭐6 Igreja de São Lourenço

The Igreja de São Lourenço ("Church of St Lawrence") sits on a tiny hill on the outskirts of Almancil. This unassuming, chalk-white building doesn't look particularly promising from the outside. If you didn't know any better, you'd just drive right past the signposted junction that leads here from the N125. If you did, you'd miss one of the most impressive churches in the Algarve. Its interior boasts a wealth of splendid azulejos.

The azulejos in the anteroom to the side of the small church can only give you a small taste of what's in store. As soon as you step inside the Igreja de São Lourenço, you'll be overwhelmed by a flood of ornamental tiles. A local legend explains why such a bastion of religious ceramics is found on this unlikely spot. It's said that the adornment of the church was arranged by some noblemen from the north of Portugal who went on a hunting trip while staying with some friends in the area. Whether or not they were fulfilling a vow or some similar commitment has been lost in the depths of time. What's certain is that the tiled decoration and the installation of the gilt high altar took place in the 18th century. The church itself has stood here since the early 1500s.

Tiles Depicting the Legend of Saint Lawrence

The church has one nave and almost no windows at all. There's nothing to distract you from the exuberant azulejos that reach all the way up into the arches and the dome. Blossoms, chalices, pomegranates, grapes, angels, garlands of flowers and many other blue-and-white patterns are just waiting to be discovered. St Lawrence, the church's namesake, appears again and again among the motifs.

According to tradition, St Lawrence served as an archdeacon under Pope Sixtus II during the Roman era and was martyred in the Italian capital in 258AD. Despite being roasted to death on a gridiron, he refused to renounce his faith to his very last breath. It is said that, shortly before being taken to be killed, he managed to share out the

---

INSIDER INFO

- If you consider yourself a Christian, you can come and **take part in the services held on Sunday morning**. You won't have to pay an entrance fee at that time. Services begin at 9am and 11am.
- You can only take photos of the Igreja de São Lourenço from the outside. **Photography and filming aren't allowed inside the building**.
- You'll usually find some **informative leaflets** at the entrance to the church.

church's riches among the poor on behalf of Sixtus, who had been executed three days before. Lawrence is venerated today as the patron saint of the destitute. He is thought to give protection against fire and offer help with eye conditions, fevers, sciatica and lumbago.

Sit and Admire

No one knows how many artists were hired to work on the decoration of the Igreja de São Lourenço, nor is it clear exactly where they got the azulejos from. None of that matters when you visit, however – just settle down on one of the wooden benches in the church's cool interior and let yourself be carried away by the beauty of the exuberant tiles.

TAKING A BREAK

You'll find the Pastelaria São Lourenço – a good place for a rest and some refreshments – on the little access road leading up to the church.

The azulejos reach right up to the rafters in the Igreja de São Lourenço. The gilded altar is typical of the 18th-century Portuguese Baroque style

🚩 204 B2   🚌 Buses to Faro, Quarteira and Loulé; www.eva-bus.com

Posto de Turismo
✉ Loja do Munícipe, Rua José dos Santos Vaquinhas, Lote 53 R/C Loja 8, Almancil   ☎ 289 400 860

Igreja de São Lourenço
🕐 Mon 3–5pm, Tue–Sat 10am–1pm and 3–5pm   🎫 €2

⭐9 Ilha da Culatra

The only way to get to this inhabited island in the Parque Natural da Ria Formosa (➤ 108) is by boat. The eastern part of the island lies to the south of Olhão (➤ 94) – the boat trip between the two points lasts about half an hour. It's even worth making the journey just to experience the watery world of the Ria Formosa natural park itself. You'll see canals, shellfish farms, birdlife and chugging fishing boats along the way.

The boats to the Ilha da Culatra stop off at the villages of Culatra and Farol. Hangares, the third hamlet on the island, is of no interest to visitors. Fishing and shellfish farming are the local population's bread and butter. **Culatra**, the largest village by far and inhabited year-round, doesn't face the open sea. Instead, it sits in a sheltered position by a lagoon. As you sail up to the village, you'll be greeted with views of one of the most picturesque fishing harbours in southern Portugal. It's a bustling place. Colourful boats, stacks of nets, fishermen at work and gulls that love to pounce on leftover bits of the day's catch all form part of the typical scene. It's interesting to note that the harbour has only existed since 2008. Before then, the locals just pulled their boats up onto the beach.

In its Own Little World
There aren't any roads or traffic lights on the Ilha da Culatra. There isn't any conventional traffic, either. As a result, you won't see any traffic jams and there's little danger to pedestrians. A few tractors and golf buggies serve as the main means of transportation. You'll also see people using the occasional wheelbarrow or a shopping trolley stolen from a supermarket. Although the mainland with its "proper" civilisation and sea of houses is almost close enough to

The lighthouse in Farol (right) shows the fishing boats (left) the way home through the Parque Natural Ria Formosa at night

reach out and touch, Culatra is a veritable world unto itself in the waters of the Ria Formosa Natural Park. About 1,000 people live here permanently. There's a school, a health centre, a library, a sports field, a few bars and eateries and a long walkway over to a flat beach surrounded by dunes. The first fishermen settled here in the late 1800s. They built some very simple huts and led a very individual lifestyle. Many of the small houses look neat and solid today – some are even built from concrete and stone. But despite these improvements, they're far from luxurious.

Farol and the Lighthouse

You should also take a stroll through the rows of houses in Farol, the second place worth seeing on the Ilha da Culatra (on the island's southwesternmost shore). Farol's most eye-catching sight is the lighthouse, a late-19th-century building that was raised to a height of 50m (165ft) in 1921. The light has a range of 50km (30mi). What's more, Farol isn't far from the beach. A trip to Culatra island is guaranteed to enchant families with kids.

TAKING A BREAK

There are several simple eateries in Culatra and Farol. **Janoca**, a café-restaurant, is a good place to go for a drink and a portion of fish or shellfish. Open year-round, it's not far from Culatra's fishing harbour.

➕ 205 D1

INSIDER INFO

- Lots of accommodation is rented out privately during the summer season. This is particularly true in Farol.
- Take care to **note the exact return times** of the ferries.
- The *Festa do Dia da Ilha*, a festival held on the 19th of July, is an important celebration on the island. Another festival takes place in August (usually the first weekend of the month) in honour of the Virgin Mary, the venerated patroness of fishermen. It's called the *Festa em Honra de Nossa Senhora dos Navegantes*.

☆10 Faro

At first glance, Faro can seem pretty confusing to visitors. After all, it's the largest city in the Algarve and home to 50,000 people (65,000 including the surrounding area). If you come armed with a plan, however, the city will start to grow on you and you'll quickly find your feet. Focus on the Old Town inside the city walls (follow signposts to the *Vila Adentro*).

The Roman settlement of *Ossonoba* is regarded as the forerunner to Faro, an important modern city that borders the Parque Natural da Ria Formosa (➤ 108) to the south. The lagoon-filled landscape of the natural park starts right on the outskirts of town, and white storks bring a touch of nature to the city. The **harbour** is a nice spot that's located in sight of the walls that surround the city's historic quarter. The best place to start exploring is from the **Arco da Vila** (➤ walk, 170), the old city gate.

Enjoy views of the city and the surrounding area from the cathedral's bell tower (above, bottom right)

Views from the Bell Tower

If you let yourself drift a little way through the partly cobbled streets, you'll come out sooner or later at the Sé, Faro's mighty **cathedral**. Originally built in the late Middle Ages, parts of the structure had to be rebuilt over the years due to a fire, looting and damage from an earthquake. Decorative tiles and an organ can be admired inside the cathedral itself. Around 70 steps lead up to the **bell tower** from the courtyard outside. Your reward for the strenuous climb is the wonderful view out over the city and the surrounding wetlands of the natural park.

Smart old townhouses line the pedestrianized Rua de Santo António

Faro has been a bishopric since 1577. The **Bishop's Palace** isn't far from the cathedral, and a monument featuring Francisco Gomes do Avilar (1739–1816) – one of the most notable representatives of a long line of church dignitaries – stands in the cathedral square. The nearby **Museu Municipal** (Municipal Museum) also has a religious heritage. It's located in the former convent of Nossa Senhora da Assunção, a beautiful 16th-century Renaissance edifice. The museum's collection focuses on archaeology, history and art. Visitors can see such exhibits as ancient columns and capitals, a large Roman mosaic, and paintings from various epochs. Several rooms are used for temporary exhibitions. Even if you're not interested in the museum itself, it's still worth checking out the building's twin-storey cloister.

A Lively Place to Live

Faro is anything but dusty and historical – it's a very lively place indeed. This is guaranteed by the **student population** who like to go out around the street known locally as the

"Rua do Crime" at night. Thanks to some good flight connections, a number of international nightlife fans have also started coming to Faro to party.

Faro & Central Algarve

The pedestrian area outside the city walls is a good place to stroll around. As you explore, you'll come across a number of inviting **cafés and restaurants**.

TAKING A BREAK

You'll find some places to eat and drink around Faro's beautiful harbour.

➕ 204 C1, City Map 202 🚌 Avenida da Républica; connections to Lagos, Loulé, Monte Gordo, Olhão, Portimão, São Brás de Alportel, Vila Real de Santo António, Lisbon and the Spanish town of Seville, etc.; www.eva-bus.com
🚆 Largo da Estação; rail connections to Lagos, Lisbon, Tavira, Vila Real de Santo António, etc.; www.cp.pt

Posto de Turismo
✉ Rua da Misericórdia 8–12 ☎ 289 803 604; www.cm-faro.pt
🕐 Daily 9am–1pm, 2pm–5/6pm

Sé (Cathedral)
✉ Largo da Sé 🕐 in summer, Mon–Fri 10am–6:30pm and Sat 9:30am–1pm; rest of the year, Mon–Fri 10am–5:30pm, Sat 9:30–1pm 🎟 €3

Museu Municipal (Municipal Museum)
✉ Praça do Afonso III 14 🕐 June–Sept, Tue–Fri 10am–7pm, Sat, Sun 11:30am–6pm; Oct–May, Tue–Fri 10am–6pm, Sat, Sun 10:30am–5pm 🎟 €2

Faro's Igreja do Carmo is famous for its Chapel of Bones

INSIDER INFO

■ You can see the cathedral without paying an entrance fee if you attend a **service**. These usually begin at 8:45am from Mon–Fri, at 6pm on Sat (9:30pm in July/Aug) and at noon on Sunday.

■ Check out the eerie **Capela dos Ossos** (Chapel of Bones). The walls and ceiling are decorated with 1,200 skulls and other parts of human skeletons. Igreja do Carmo, Largo do Carmo, Mon–Fri 10–1pm & 3–6pm, Sat 10am–1pm, €2.

⑳ Vilamoura

A marina of this size is a rarity and makes Vilamoura a little bit special. Bars, bistros, lounges and restaurants huddle together around the water. There's always a great atmosphere.

Celebs, business moguls and people who like to see and be seen flock to the terrace cafés at Vilamoura's marina

The marina in Vilamoura boasts space for an impressive 825 boats, making it one of the largest harbours in southern Portugal. The water is surrounded by a variety of restaurants, bars and shops. Portuguese footballing legend Luis Figo once successfully invested in a business here (the Sete Café), and the area is still a good place for celebrity sightings. The same goes for the golf courses nearby. Mere mortals can vicariously soak up some of the highlife by taking a stroll around the marina itself, where you'll witness an appealing contrast between the chicest of the chic and down-to-earth living. Whether or not you want to eat at the marina is up to you – the prices are slightly more expensive than elsewhere, but its big terraces make it much more atmospheric.

Vilamoura was built in the 1970s to cater to the rise of tourism. It's blighted with a number of crimes against architecture as a result. Depending on the time of year, there's a lot to see and do here. That's particularly true of the marina, dubbed the "Best Marina in Portugal".

TAKING A BREAK

One thing can be said of Vilamoura's marina: there's no shortage of places to eat and drink! Find somewhere with just the right level of busyness, atmosphere, price and sunshine to suit your tastes, and settle down to enjoy some refreshments.

🕂 201 F2 ℹ️ www.marinadevilamoura.com

㉑ Albufeira

Albufeira, a city of around 25,000 inhabitants, is geared to mass tourism with its busy city centre, its great beaches, its marina and its heady summer living during the day and at night. The hustle and bustle here isn't typical of the Algarve – just bear that in mind before you visit.

There are many different sides to Albufeira, a holiday resort that boasts 15km (9mi) of coast. This makes it difficult to sum up in one go. As you might expect, the best destinations are scattered throughout the area. The west is home to a marina with nearly 500 berths and beaches like the **Praia do Castelo**. Way out east is the **Praia da Falésia** (➤ 92), a

INSIDER INFO

Boat tours set off from the marina on yachts and catamarans. Providers include Algarve Charters (tel. 289 314 867; www.algarvecharters.com).

The Praia dos Pescadores: once the domain of fishermen, the beach is now a popular tourist destination

landscape filled with cliffs and top hotels. If you want to visit the city centre, head to the Largo Engenheiro Duarte Pacheco. It's an ideal starting point for discovering the pedestrian streets with their many bars and souvenir shops.

A tunnel leads from the Rua 5 de Outobro to Albufeira's favourite local beach, the **Praia dos Pescadores**. The tide of tourists ebbs a little if you head to the upper part of town, where you'll find the Igreja Matriz, the Ermida de São Sebastião (on the Praça Miguel Bombarda) and the Igreja de Sant'Ana. All three of these churches date back to the 18th century. The Torre do Relógio, the clock tower of the former district jail, is another of Albufeira's eye-catching sights.

TAKING A BREAK

It's worth making a detour to the marina in the western part of the city – you'll find a number of terraces where you can enjoy a refreshing drink.

Insider Tip

🕂 201 D2 🚌 Alto dos Caliços; connections to Almancil, Faro, Lagoa, Lisbon, Portimão, Silves, etc.; www.eva-bus.com

Posto de Turismo
✉ Rua 5 de Outobro ☎ 289 585 279; www.cm-albufeira.pt 🕐 9–1 and 2–5/6

At Your Leisure

Cosy streets in Fuseta (image above); a procession in honour of Loulé's patron saints (➤ 112, image right)

22 Fuseta

An unassuming country highway branches off to Fuseta from the N125 between Olhão and Tavira. This nice, authentic village used to consist of a couple of fishing huts. As it developed, the locals started building cube-shaped houses that stand out today thanks to their characteristic chimneys and roof terraces. Fuseta's location by the lagoon-filled landscape of the Parque Natural da Ria Formosa (➤ 108) makes it an attractive place for visitors.

Fuseta – which is also sometimes spelled "Fuzeta" (don't get confused!) – is home to lots of people who still make a living from fishing. They supply the many little local restaurants that serve some excellent seafood.

Fishing boats moor in the deep, narrow port. A wide, flat, sandy beach on the outskirts of the village slopes gently down into the waters of the lagoon. A large campsite lies a short way behind the lagoon itself. Head along the promenade to the harbour to watch the comings and goings of the fishing boats. Boat shuttle services and water taxis regularly travel over to the long **Praia da Fuseta** – a nice place for a day trip! More extensive boat tours through the Parque Natural da Ria Formosa set off from the harbour. The operator there goes

Faro & Central Algarve

BARFLIES

The **Bar O Farol** sits very close to the lagoon on the Rua Professor César Oliveira in Fuseta. Find yourselves a spot out on the roomy terrace and relax with a refreshing drink. Now and then, the bar plays host to live concerts and local DJs (mostly on Wednesday and Saturday evenings). You'll usually find information about these events by having a look on the bar's Facebook page (tel. 936 064 369).

by the name of Passeios Ria Formosa (tel. 962 156 922; www.passeios-ria-for mosa.com). Most of the trips include a stop at the **Praia do Homem Nú**, a secluded lagoon beach.
✚ 205 E2

23 Parque Natural da Ria Formosa

Measuring in at 18,400ha (45,000 acres) in size, the Parque Natural da Ria Formosa is one of the natural wonders of Portugal. Boasting a width of over 60km (37mi), this nature park runs along the coast from a point to the west of Faro to a spot near **Manta Rota** (➤ 79) in the eastern Algarve. It's characterised by its lagoons, its inhabited and uninhabited islands and its canals, all of which are affected by the strong Atlantic tides. The islands with their long, sandy beaches act as natural barriers against the sea.

The nature reserve is a pretty special place. One minute, you'll feel as if you're in the middle of nowhere, then all of a sudden you'll turn a corner and see vast numbers of houses and the airport in Faro just a stone's throw away. Fishing and shellfish farming are important sources of income for the local population. The park is also home to **oyster farms** that supply customers in France. You haven't got a hope of getting your hands on them – the oysters, which mature in the nutrient-rich waters for six to twelve months, are sold long in advance. With all this economic activity going on, you might have guessed that the park isn't exactly devoid of human influence. Nevertheless, it still provides a habitat for numerous species of bird, including flamingos, herons, gulls and shags (part of the cormorant family). It also boasts one of Europe's most significant colonies of seahorses.

The largest islands in the natural park are the Ilha de Tavira (➤ 80), the Ilha da Armona (➤ 95), the Ilha da Culatra (➤ 98) and the Ilha Deserta. They're all open to visitors. Lots of fishermen live on the Ilha da Culatra, while the Ilha Deserta is pretty deserted (as its name might suggest!) The inhabited Ilha de Faro (➤ 110) with its long, sandy beach can be reached by car if you drive over the bridge to the west of Faro. The other islands are free of traffic (except for the tractors that serve as transportation on Culatra). Both locals and visitors alike have to rely on boats and water taxis as a result. Boats regularly travel to the Ilha de Tavira from **Tavira** (➤ 66), and head to the Ilha da Armona, the Ilha da Culatra and the Ilha Deserta from **Olhão** (➤ 94). You can also sail to the islands from the villages of Cabanas de Tavira (➤ 63, 109, 179) and Santa Luzia (➤ 80).
✚ 205 D1

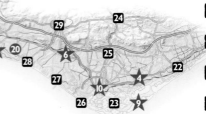

A flower decoration for the Feast of Corpus Christi in São Brás de Alportel

24 São Brás de Alportel

It's worth making a detour to this small country town just to visit the **Museu do Traje**, a museum that's largely (but not exclusively) dedicated to local costume. The museum building is interesting in its own right. The collection is housed in a palace that was built in the 19th century by a former mule driver who had the economic foresight to prosper from the cork trade and the local cork industry. The building greets you with a pretty courtyard and its azulejos-covered facades. The permanent collection, which usually displays a selection of regional costumes from the Algarve, is changed around every couple of years. An elongated courtyard stretches out behind the building. Coaches stand under protective roofs and you can explore the former stables that contain an informative display about cork (➤ 20). The courtyard is also home to the Bar Cantinho do Museu, which serves meals and is a good place for a breather. The Museu do Traje also acts as a local cultural centre. Sunday is typically a good day to hear some fado or jazz or see some traditional dance.

It's a good idea to find out about the dates and times of performances in advance. It doesn't take very long to see the rest of this little town of 12,000 inhabitants. The historic centre with its tiled facades and the Igreja Matriz (begun in the 15th century) is rather modest. Cork oaks grow all around São

BOAT TOURS IN THE NATURAL PARK

The best way to really get to grips with exploring the Parque Natural da Ria Formosa is on an organised boat tour. Families with kids will love them, too. Tours range from an hour-long jaunt to a whole-day adventure. There are several tour providers, including Passeios Ria Formosa (tel. 962 156 922; www.passeios-ria-formosa.com), who have bases in Olhão (➤ 94), Fuseta (➤ 106), Cabanas de Tavira (➤ 68) and Santa Luzia (➤ 80). They offer all the usual round trips alongside some more specialised bird-watching and seahorse tours. If you want to get around under your own steam, exercise your muscles and feel much more in harmony with nature, it might also be a good idea to venture out on a sea kayak trip!

Insider Tip

Brás de Alportel, and several cork factories still operate in the area.
➕ 205 D3 🚌 Rua João Louro; connections to Faro; www.eva-bus.com

Posto de Turismo
✉ Largo de São Sebastião 23
☎ 289 843 165; www.cm-sbras.pt

Museu do Traje
✉ Rua Dr. José Dias Sancho 61 ☎ 289 840 100;
www.museu-sbras.com 🕐 Mon–Fri 10am–1pm
and Mon–Sun 2pm–5pm 💶 €2

25 Milreu

Visit the Ruínas Romanas de Milreu to see the remains of Roman buildings dating from the 1st to the 4th century AD. They once formed part of a *Villa Rustica*, a typical villa complex from where people used to keep tabs on the agricultural and livestock industries in the area. Wine and olives were among the most important crops back then. These have given way to oranges and almond trees today. Take a walk around the site and you'll spot several interesting mosaics with fish motifs, the remains of a brick temple and fragments of free-standing pillars. Parts of Roman walls and mosaics can also be seen inside the adjacent building, the Casa Rural de Milreu.

The Milreu site is small, clearly set out and easy to explore. The entrance lies around 600m away from the centre of Estoi on the road to Faro.
➕ 204 C2
☎ 289 997 823 www.monumentosdoalgarve.pt
🕐 May–Sep, Tue–Sun 9:30–1, 2–6:30;
Oct–Apr, Tue–Sun 9–1, 2–5:30 💶 €2

26 Ilha de Faro

You'll have to pass the noisy international airport to get here, but don't let that put you off – the Ilha de Faro, an island belonging to the Parque Natural da Ria Formosa (▶ 108), is definitely still worth the trip. If you've come by car, you won't have to take a boat to get to

THE PALACE OF ESTOI

The Palace of Estoi is the most significant structure in the village of Estoi. Originally built at the end of the 18th century, it sits near the Roman ruins of Milreu. The palace and gardens were first restored from 1893–1909. It was later restored again around the turn of the century, when architects added a series of modern walls that seem somewhat out-of-keeping with the original design. It's now home to one of the Pousada chain of hotels. They've preserved the palace's stylish salons, a romantic garden and one of the facades. You're allowed to have a look around, even if you're not staying or eating at the hotel (▶ 115).

Insider Tip

the island – simply drive across the bridge. When you reach the other side, you'll find yourself in the densely developed middle part of this extremely narrow landmass. The further you venture away from this central area, the more authentic everything becomes. If you head off the beaten track, you'll spot a number of interesting fishermen's houses, some of which can only be reached over boardwalks. The long, sandy **Praia de Faro** faces towards the sea and is an inviting spot for swimming, sunbathing and strolling. The island is also home to a number of restaurants.
➕ 204 C1

27 Quinta do Lago

Quinta do Lago, one of the classiest and most exclusive destinations in the Algarve, is located a short way south of Almancil. The moneyed elite enjoy hanging out in its villas, golf courses, holiday homes and such classy five-star hotels as the Conrad (www.conradalgarve.com) and the Quinta do Lago (www.hotel quintadolago.com). You'll sometimes spot celebrities here – it's no accident that Quinta do Lago has been called the "Beverly Hills of Portugal".

If you prefer something more down-to-earth, the surrounding area is also home to hiking and cycling routes that let you explore parts of the wetlands in the Parque Natural da Ria Formosa (➤ 108). It's also a favourite spot for the birdwatchers who come here in the early morning hours.

Locals and active holiday-makers also enjoy heading down to Quinta do Lago's lake, where you'll find a popular water sports centre. The activities on offer include windsurfing, kayaking and pedalo rides (tel. 289 394 929; www.lagowatersports.com).

Water sports fans will also find lots of fun things to do on the long, sandy **Praia da Quinta do Lago** beach that stretches out alongside the Atlantic.

✚ 204 B1

Great for a stroll: the Ria Formosa's salt marshes near Quinta do Lago

28 Quarteira

Once a modest fishing village, Quarteira was developed and concreted over as much as possible during the seaside tourism boom that kicked off in the 1960s. As a result, it's not exactly beautiful, but the fishing port and the traditional fish market hall still keep some of its old flair alive. There are several fish restaurants. Quarteira hosts the **Fisherman's festival** *(Dia do Pescador)* at the end of May. The promenade along the stretches of sandy beach nearby is handsomely appointed, and the Praia do Forte Novo outside town is a beautiful beach destination.

➕ 201 F2

29 Loulé

Although it was a centre of Moorish life in the Middle Ages, Loulé

> **GET READY TO PARTY...**
>
> The most important dates for the party-mad folk of Loulé are the **carneval** and the **Festa da Mãe Soberana**, two events that are famous far beyond the Algarve's borders. The latter festival begins on Easter Sunday and finishes two weeks later. The MED world music festival is held at the end of June. Don't hesitate if you want to experience one of these events – they fill up fast.

largely missed out on the profits from both the Age of Discovery and tourism due to its out-of-the-way location. Despite this, it's carved out a niche as the most important hub in the surrounding agricultural area. It's a good place to visit just for its **market hall** alone. *Insider Tip*

The neo-Moorish market hall – part of everyday life in Loulé

This eye-catching neo-Moorish building plays host to a forest of stalls that are well worth exploring. You can buy sweet treats made from almonds and figs, chutneys, wines and little bags of herbs. There's also an abundant selection of fruit and vegetables on offer. The biggest crowds of people come on Saturday mornings, when the stands spill outside and surround the hall. Dive in and enjoy!

Loulé's most significant, historical buildings are spread out around the city. The **Igreja Matriz de São Clemente** (13th c.), the late Gothic main church on the Largo Batalhão Sapadores Caminhos de Ferro, was originally a mosque. It's also worth visiting the area around the small, turreted castle complex near the Largo de Dom Pedro I. This **castelo** dates back to the Middle Ages. A set of stairs lead up into the tower. The lower section of the castle is home to the **Museu Municipal de Arqueologia** (Municipal Archaeological Museum) and the *Cozinha Tradicional*, a typical Algarve country kitchen. Head back to the street you turned off to get to the castle and you'll come across the **Ermida de Nossa Senhora da Conceição**. Although easily overlooked, this small church is home to a surprisingly fancy interior filled with splendid azulejos and Baroque ornamentation. If you prefer something more modern, go to the domed **Santuario de Nossa Senhora da Piedade**, a sanctuary of the Virgin Mary that stands on a hill outside the city.

🕂 204 B3 🚌 Rua Nossa Senhora de Fátima; connections to Albufeira, Alte, Armação de Pêra, Faro, Lagoa, Loulé, Portimão, São Bras de Alportel, etc.; www.eva-bus.com

Posto de Turismo
✉ Avenida 25 de Abril 9
☎ 289 463 900; www.cm-loule.pt

Castelo
(with the Museu Municipal de Arqueologia and the Cozinha Tradicional)
✉ Rua de Paio Peres Correia
🕐 Mon–Fri 9:30–5:30, Sat 9:30–4 💳 €2

Ermida de Nossa Senhora da Conceição
✉ Rua de Paio Peres Correia
🕐 Tue–Fri 9:30–5:30, Sat 9:30–4 💳 Free

🔟 Alte

When you're driving to Alte, bear this old saying in mind: the journey is better than the destination. The trip is only worth making if you want to take the trouble to explore the inland Algarve, a region filled with pomegranate and orange trees and the undulating hills of the Serra do Caldeirão. The pace of life here is different from what you'll see on the coast – it's a great place to relax and enjoy your holiday.

Alte is a peaceful village with whitewashed houses, a church on the square and its very own natural spring. The tranquillity of village life is disrupted once a year when Alte plays host to a riotous carnival.

If you've approached Alte from the northwest via **São Bartolomeu de Messines**, carry on your tour by driving past **Benafim** and **Salir** to the east of the village. You'll get some more impressions of typical rural life along the way – something you won't see when you reach **Loulé** (► 112) and the coast.
🕂 204 B3

Where to...
Stay

Prices
for a double room per night in the high season
€ under 90 euros   €€ 90–150 euros   €€€ over 150 euros

ALBUFEIRA

Epic Sana €€€

You'll be met by a gigantic, airy foyer as you step into this high-class, achingly modern, service-orientated hotel surrounded by pine woods and 8ha (20 acres) of grounds. Apart from the well-equipped hotel rooms, it also boasts a special complex with apartments that are ideal for 🏨 families with kids. This level of luxury comes at a price. The main building is home to a large indoor swimming pool and a gym, which guests can use round the clock. They charge extra for the smaller indoor pool, the sauna and the steam room. There's also an attractive gourmet restaurant and some appealing outdoor spaces. A short footpath outside the hotel grounds leads to the Praia da Falésia. The hotel is located in the east of Albufeira.

🏨 201 E2 ✉ Pinhal do Concelho, Praia da Falésia, Olhos d'Água ☎ 289 104 300; www.algarve.epic.sanahotels.com

Pine Cliffs Resort €€€

This resort provides exclusivity of the highest order – something that's reflected in the price. They offer exceptional accommodation in a spacious, hermetically sealed-off site above the Praia da Falésia that's filled with lawns and umbrella pines. As well as its health club, pool areas and top gastronomic destinations, the resort is also home to the prestigious Algarve Sheraton hotel.

🏨 201 E2 ✉ Pinhal do Concelho, Praia da Falésia, Olhos d'Água ☎ 289 500 300; www.pinecliffs.com

Quinta do Mel €€–€€€

Country house accommodation with a pool in an old feudal manor. It's located along the route to Vilamoura marina in the eastern-most part of Albufeira (N.B. it isn't by the sea). A great place for anyone who wants to relax and get to know the inland Algarve. The prices vary immensely – it can even drop into the € price category outside the high season.

🏨 201 E2 ✉ Olhos d'Água
☎ 289 543 674; www.quintadomel.com

Sheraton Algarve €€€

This is without doubt one of the most beautiful hotel complexes to be found anywhere in the Algarve. Its spacious, lush green site stretches out behind the cliffs along the coast to the east of Albufeira. The rooms are lavishly furnished. 🏨 Families with kids will also feel welcome here – children up to 8 years of age can be let loose on the large Porto Pirata play area. All guests are free to make use of the open-air and indoor pools, the fitness room, the O Pescador restaurant and the Piri Piri Steak House. You can take the hotel's own elevator or walk down the stairs to the Falésia, a lengthy beach that stretches out along the cliff-lined coast.

🏨 201 E2
✉ Praia da Falésia
☎ 289 500 100; www.sheratonalgarve.com

LOULÉ

Loulé Coreto Hostel €
Simple, low-priced accommodation that's off the beaten track – it's located away from the coast and the centre of Loulé. If this sounds like an appealing combination, you'll enjoy staying here. Wall paintings, wooden floors and colourful curtains make the rooms feel fresh and comfortable. The cheapest place to sleep is in a bed in one of the shared rooms or dormitories (guests are separated according to gender). You'll get to meet like-minded people in the communal kitchen and if you venture out onto the roof terrace. The large majority of guests are young.

➕ 204 B3
✉ Avenida José da Costa Mealha 68
☎ 966 660 943; http://loulecoretohostel.com

OLHÃO

Casa Modesta €€
Family-run country house accommodation. It's pretty comfortable. They combine a contemporary atmosphere with the history of Joaquim Modesto de Brito, the old sea dog who set the place up. You'll come face to face with nature in the surrounding Parque Natural da Ria Formosa. There's a minimum stay of two nights at some times of the year.

➕ 205 D1
✉ Quatrim do Sul
☎ 964 738 824; www.casamodesta.pt

Real Marina Hotel & Spa €€€
The only five-star hotel in Olhão. It's located in the western part of town. Although the building itself is a giant, modern block, its facilities include several pools, a spa, a sun terrace and the Ria Lounge restaurant and bar. It's also within walking distance of the town centre. The promenade opposite leads past the offshoots of the Parque Natural da Ria Formosa on its way to the market halls. The hotel's prices usually drop into the € category during the low season.

➕ 205 D1
✉ Avenida 5 de Outubro
☎ 289 091 300; www.real-marina.com

Where to...
Eat and Drink

Prices
for a three-course set menu without drinks or service
€ under 20 euros   €€ 20–35 euros   €€€ over 35 euros

ALBUFEIRA

La Joya €€€
Dining at this temple to the culinary arts costs a three-figure sum. Home to Austrian chef Dieter Koschina, the restaurant holds two Michelin stars. Arnaud, the hugely knowledgeable sommelier, will help you find the right wine.

➕ 201 D2 ✉ Estrada da Galé
☎ 289 591 795; www.vilajoya.com
🕐 Daily noon–2:30pm, 7pm–10:30pm
(times may vary)

ESTOI

Pousada Palácio de Estoi €€€
This restaurant in a Pousada hotel stands out thanks to its tasteful

atmosphere – it feels as thought it's been steeped in the aura of the former palace it calls home (► box, 110). The chefs create regional cuisine cooked to a very high standard. It's worth checking out the garden and the historic salons *(Salão Nobre, Salão Verde)* before or after you dine. If you like, you can also spend the night in one of the beautiful Pousada's 63 rooms.

➕ 204 C2 ✉ Rua São José
☎ 289 990 150; www.pestana.com
🕐 12:30–3pm and 7pm–10pm

FARO

Vivmar €€

It's no surprise that the menu here is dominated by fish and seafood – it's run by a fishing association, after all! This eatery with a rustic touch looks pretty inconspicuous. It sits right outside the city walls near the Centro Ciência Viva do Algarve.

➕ 204 C1 ✉ Rua Comandante Francisco Manuel 8 ☎ 916 145 584
🕐 Mon–Sat noon–3pm & 7pm–10pm

FUSETA

Casa A. Corvo €

Insider Tip

This simple restaurant is a true institution in Fuseta that's very popular with the locals. You'll sometimes have to wait, but it's worth exercising a little patience to try out the excellent fish from the grill. The quality of the food is as extraordinary as the low prices. Don't expect any meticulous cleanliness, however. Everything's grilled right next to the terrace where you eat.

➕ 205 E2 ✉ Largo 1° de Maio 33
☎ 918 928 785 🕐 times vary, generally Tue–Sat noon–3pm & 7pm–10:30pm

ILHA DA CULATRA

A do João €–€€

An island restaurant on Culatra in the village of Farol (also home to a lighthouse). It's known for its fresh fish and typical seafood dishes. Some lovely places to sit outside.

➕ 205 D1
✉ Ilha da Culatra, right on the beach
☎ 289 714 209; www.adojoao.com
🕐 high season: daily 12–12

LOULÉ

11 da Villa €

This popular, atmospheric gastro-pub enjoys a nice location on a pleasant square in Loulé's historic Old Town. You can grab a seat outside or find yourself a cosy spot in the grotto-like brick interior. It's a good place to enjoy a drink or two and try out a few of the snacks on offer.

➕ 204 B3 ✉ Largo de D. Pedro I.
☎ 919 557 268; www.merceariagourmet.com
🕐 Tue–Thu 11am–11pm, Fri, Sat 11am–1am

Café Calcinha €

This traditional coffee house, which dates back to the late 1920s, was originally built to mimic the style of a Brazilian coffee shop. It's a popular hangout for locals and visitors alike. A bronze figure depicting António Aleixo (1899–1949), a local poet who died in Loulé, stands outside. You can sit inside or find a seat out on the terrace.

➕ 204 B3 ✉ Praça da República 67
☎ 289 415 763 🕐 Mon–Fri 11–10, Sat 11–4

Museu do Lagar €€

This typical, rustic restaurant serving regional specialties occupies the site of a former olive oil mill *(lagar)* – something attested to by the tools and implements you'll see inside. It's situated in the square in front of the Igreja Matriz de São Clemente. The small terrace is separated from the car park by a row of plant pots. Live music is often performed on Friday evenings.

➕ 204 B3 ✉ Largo Batalhão Sapadores/Caminhos de Ferro 7/8 ☎ 289 422 718
🕐 Mon–Sat noon–3pm & 7pm–11pm

OLHÃO

O Bote €€

This eatery is considered one of the best seafood and fish restaurants in town, largely thanks to its specialities from the grill. You'll find it a short way away from the market halls. It's always busy, but there are lots of other places to eat on the same street if you can't get a table.

➕ 205 D1
✉ Avenida 5 de Outubro 122
☎ 289 721 183
🕐 noon–3pm & 7pm–10:30pm

Where to...
Shop

Markets and flea markets are worth a visit even if you just want to browse. The market halls in Olhão and Loulé – two of the most beautiful examples of their kind in southern Portugal – are particularly colourful and atmospheric on Saturday mornings, when numerous stalls pop up outside. Loulé is considered a centre for arts and crafts, while Olhão and Faro boast large shopping centres.

FRUIT, VEGETABLES, HANDICRAFTS

You'll find an abundance of fresh **fruit and vegetables** at the markets alongside a selection of fish, cheese, spices, etc. Various stalls in Loulé also sell wine and extremely nutritious sweet baked goods made from almonds, figs and carob pods. They also offer such handicrafts as lace doilies and pottery. Loulé enjoys an excellent reputation for **ceramics**. You'll spot fine examples of this handiwork if you head to the shops in the small town centre – make

sure to check out Teresa's Pottery (Largo Dom Pedro I. 15) that sells hand-painted plates and coffee cups. The current trend is for sophisticated designer ceramics, but traditional goods made from rush wickerwork – including such useful items as baskets, hats and door mats – are also still produced in the region surrounding the city.

SHOPPING CENTRES

Ria Shopping/Algarve Outlet (www.algarveoutlet.pt), a mall near Olhão, caters to a completely different crowd: it's usually open until 11pm (midnight in August). The Forum Algarve (www.forum algarve.net) lies on the northwestern outskirts of Faro. The Portuguese love this kind of **shopping centre**, especially as they can eat and watch movies there, too.

SHOP 'TIL YOU DROP

The centre of **Albufeira** is a great place to shop, but the cookie-cutter souvenir stands are faceless and impersonal. **Faro** is ideal for window shopping. You'll find most of the stores outside the Old Town – check out the shops in and around such streets as the Rua de Santo António.

DATES

Flea and junk markets (feiras de velharias) are extremely popular events. It's worth checking out the following: Albufeira, 2nd and 3rd Saturday of the month (Mercado Municipal dos Caliços); Olhos d'Água, 1st Sunday of the month; the centre of Quarteira, 1st Saturday of the month; Fuseta (right by the campsite), 2nd Sunday of the month; and São Brás de Alportel (Parque Roberto Nobre), 3rd Sunday of the month. Ask at a tourist office to find out about the latest dates.

Where to...
Go Out

The central Algarve is a fantastic place for anyone who loves having some fun after the sun goes down. Vilamoura marina is a perennial favourite that pretty much guarantees you a good time. Otherwise, you'll find the best atmosphere in Faro and the Albufeira holiday district.

HOTSPOTS: ALBUFEIRA & FARO

If you're in Albufeira and fancy going out to party, head to the Avenida Dr. Francisco Sá Carneiro (a.k.a. the **"Albufeira Strip"**). Things often don't really start to hot up here until after midnight in summer. It also gets very lively indeed around the **Largo Engenheiro Duarte Pacheco** in the centre of town. People love to go dancing at the Lounge Garden in the T-Clube nightclub (www.tclube.com) in Quinta do Lago on Saturday nights (on Buganvilia Plaza near the Quinta do Lago shopping centre).

Faro's nightlife benefits from the city's student population. They're generally welcoming and love having foreign visitors around. The most popular place to go out at night is known as the **Rua do Crime** (the "street of crime"). This is just the local nickname for the area around the Rua do Prior, so don't try and find it on a map!

DO AS THE LOCALS DO

Lots of young party animals in the central Algarve flock to the **Discotheca Kadoc** (Cerca da Areia; www.kadoc.pt), a venue that calls itself the "largest Disco Club in the Algarve" (no one's yet come forward to prove otherwise!)

Cinemas can be found in such shopping centres as the Forum Algarve (www.forumalgarve.net) on Faro's northwestern outskirts. Locals and visiting culture fans enjoy heading to the **theatre** in Faro – check out the Teatro das Figuras (Horta das Figuras, tel. 289 888 100; www.teatrodasfiguras.pt) or the Teatro Lethes (Rua de Portugal 58, tel. 289 878 908; www.actateatro.org.pt/teatrolethes).

LEISURE ACTIVITIES

Without doubt, the region's most popular sporting activities are golf and water sports of all imaginable shapes and sizes. The **selection of water sports** on offer ranges from standup paddleboarding to kite surfing. Operators include Kite Culture Algarve (tel. 919 318 820; www.kite-algarve..com). Their HQ is in Fuseta.

The Algarve's **golf courses** tend to be located in the centre of the region. Oceânico Pinhal (Vilamoura; www.oceanicogolf.com) and Pinheiros Altos (Sítio dos Pinheiros, Quinta do Lago; www.pinheirosaltos.com) number among the best-known links in the area.

FUN OR FAUNA & FLORA

The **boat trips** on offer at the marinas in Albufeira and Vilamoura make for some great holiday experiences. They're also meant to be a bit of fun – passengers are encouraged to kick back and enjoy a drink or three on board. If you'd rather spend your time exploring the natural world, sign up for a nature boat trip or a sea kayak tour through the Parque Natural da Ria Formosa.

The "Algarve Guia/Guide" is published every month and can be picked up free from tourist information centres. It has information about festivals, exhibitions, sports fixtures, etc.

Insider Tip

Western Algarve

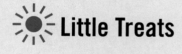

Little Treats

Sunset at the Cape

The **Cabo de São Vicente** (➤ 127) is always spectacular, but it's a particularly magnificent sight when the the sun sinks below the horizon.

All the Fun of the Market

Check out the sights (and smells!) of the market hall in **Lagos** (➤ 135). The fish stalls in the lower section are impressive.

A Twitcher's Paradise

Bring some binoculars and a camera and find a good spot by the **Lagoa dos Salgados** (➤ 139) – it's a great place for bird-watching.

Getting Your Bearings

The western Algarve is part of the Barlavento Algarvio (the "Windward Algarve"), a region of spectacular cliffs, beaches and headlands, bizarre caves and natural arches. Particularly impressive stretches of coast await you near Carvoeiro and the Ponta da Piedade by Lagos. If you're organising your own trip, you'll love such small holiday destinations as Luz and Burgau. Birdwatchers will enjoy the lookout points on the Ria de Alvor and the Lagoa dos Salgados near Armação de Pêra.

Bird-watchers should bring their binoculars

Lagos is the most beautiful, lively, historic city in the western Algarve. In contrast, the built-up towns of **Portimão** and **Armação de Pêra** can seem off-putting at first. There isn't a continuous road running along the coast, so

you'll often have to drive down side roads to get to beaches and seaside towns. Some beaches can only be reached via narrow tracks or steep stairways through the rock. The region's westernmost point is the **Ponta de Sagres** and the **Cabo de São Vicente**, a headland that's whipped by the wind and rain. Travel inland and you'll hit the **Serra de Monchique**, a leafy mountain range that shelters the area from northern winds. Fóia, its highest point, stands at 902m (2,960ft).

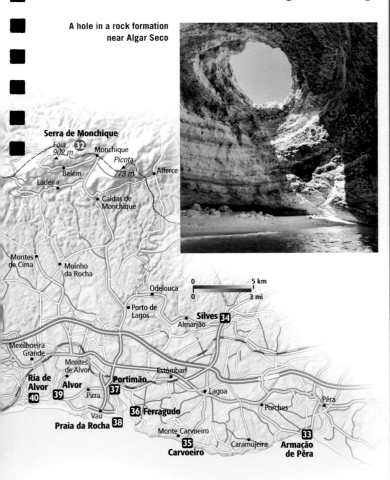

A hole in a rock formation near Algar Seco

Serra de Monchique
Fóia **32** Monchique
902 m *Picota*
Belém *773 m* Alferce
Ladeira
Caldas de Monchique
Montes de Cima
Moinho da Rocha
Odelouca
Porto de Lagos
Silves 34
Almarjão
Mexilhoeira Grande
Montes de Alvor Estômbar
Ria de Alvor Alvor **Portimão**
40 **39** Pirra **37** Lagoa
Vau **36 Ferragudo** Porches Pêra
Praia da Rocha 38 Monte Carvoeiro
35 Caramujeira **33**
Carvoeiro **Armação de Pêra**

0 — 5 km
0 — 3 mi

Perfect Days in...

Three Perfect Days

The western Algarve is a region of contrasts. We've planned an appropriately varied three-day itinerary to make sure you get to witness its diversity. The tour is a wonderful mix of cliff-lined coasts, beaches, towns, cultural sights and mountains that's guaranteed to please. You'll need a (rental) car to get around.

Day One

Morning
Spend the morning in **31 Lagos** (➤ 132) – the best base for exploring the area. (Get out as early as you can and beat the crowds by booking a boat trip to the sea caves of the Ponta da Piedade for later on.) Your first port of call in the city is the Igreja de Santo António with its magnificent azulejos and adjoining museum. Check out the small castle, the monument to Prince Henry the Navigator on the Praça do Infante Dom Henrique, and what's left of the city walls. Then set off on that boat trip to the ★ **Ponta da Piedade** (➤ 124) you booked earlier. Have lunch in Lagos afterwards.

Afternoon/Evening
Take a trip out west to the Fortaleza in **Sagres** (➤ 129) and the ★ **Cabo de São Vicente**

Serra de Monchique **32**

Silves **34**

Ria de Alvor *Alvor* **40** **39** *Portimão* **37**

Lagos **31** *Praia da Rocha* **38** **36** *Ferragudo* **35** *Carvoeiro* **33** *Armação de Pêra*

Burgau **42** *Luz* **41** ★ *Ponta da Piedade*

★ *Cabo de São Vicente* **43** *Sagres*

(➤ 127), a headland marked by wild, grandiose scenery. If you'd like to watch some fishermen at work, make a detour to the harbour in **43 Sagres** (image right). On your way back to Lagos, it's worth paying a visit to **42 Burgau** (➤ 145) and **41 Luz** (➤ 145), two nice holiday resorts with attractive beaches. They're also good places to enjoy an evening meal.

Day Two

Morning
Venture inland away from the coast. Your first stop is the **32 Serra de Monchique** (➤ 136). Drive up Fóia – at 902m (2,960ft), it's the loftiest point in the Algarve. The views are often better in the morning. On the way back, you might like to pop in to the church in **Monchique** (➤ 137). Have lunch in the spa town of **Caldas de Monchique** (➤ 137).

Afternoon
Drive further on to **34 Silves** (➤ 140) and visit the fortress that dates from the Moorish era.

Evening
Your best option this evening is to head into the Old Town of **31 Lagos** (➤ 132) for a bite to eat. It's a great place to soak up the atmosphere – the city boasts some lively nightlife in the summer.

Day Three

Morning
Today's destination is the eastern part of the western Algarve. Head to **37 Portimão** (➤ 143) on the Rio Arade. It's worth paying a visit to the museum that's housed in a former fish cannery. Then drive to the beach town of **35 Carvoeiro** (➤ 141). Have a stroll around, cool off in the Atlantic and enjoy a spot of lunch.

Afternoon
In the afternoon, head to the **Nossa Senhora da Rocha** (➤ 140) pilgrimage chapel, the sprawling sandy beach at **33 Armação de Pêra** (➤ 139) and the **Lagoa dos Salgados** (➤ 139), a landscape filled with birdlife. Birdwatchers should bring their binoculars.

Evening
Round out your day in **39 Alvor** (➤ 144), where you'll find a few restaurants for an evening meal along the **40 Ria de Alvor** (➤ 145).

Western Algarve

⭐Ponta da Piedade

The Ponta da Piedade – a headland around 2km (1.25mi) south of Lagos that juts out far into the Atlantic – is regarded as one of the most breath-taking cliff landscapes in southwest Europe. It's home to some captivatingly awesome rock formations whose bizarre beauty can only truly be appreciated on a boat tour. If that wasn't enough, it also boasts some small sections of beach and a sprinkling of rocky islands by the coast.

Wind and waves have carved the stone formations of the Ponta da Piedade into huge sculptures that have become icons of the **greater Lagos area** and symbols of the Algarve as a whole. No advertising brochure for this sun-baked region would be complete without a photo of this rocky stretch of coast. Walking along the path above the cliffs only lets you appreciate part of its grandeur – the best views can be enjoyed from the sea. Clamber aboard a popular **excursion boat** or a **sea kayak** if you're feeling adventurous.

Insider Tip

Fantastic Rock Formations

As soon as you catch sight of the shapes carved into the rock, your imagination will take flight, spurred on by vivid suggestions from the sailors who help the day roll on at a leisurely pace. Before you know it, the towers, spikes and domes in the rock will start to look like over-sized axes and gigantic animals (a cat's head, a gorilla, a hawk, an elephant, a sleeping camel…), the elaborate icing on a wedding cake, Pinocchio with his long nose, the famous Titanic, the beautiful Arc de Triomphe in Paris, and the noble, crowned head of a Queen. Holes in the cliffs that bear a striking resemblance to eerie eye sockets will make you do a double take. The combination of rocks and the sea here creates a **magical landscape** that's been eroded, eaten away and shaped as if by an invisible hand.

Sea Caves and the Play of Natural Light

Another highlight is when the boats head **through the rock arches and into the caves**. These stone labyrinths filled with spikes and sharp edges have to be navigated with utmost care. Don't worry, the sailors know exactly what they're doing. They're trained to make complicated manoeuvres to deal with the swell of the waves and the sea as it foams, gargles, swirls and undulates in the caverns. Depending on the time of day and the sun, the caves can be flooded with blue-green light effects that look like artificial illuminations. Vertical tunnels in the rock open up to the sky above, and the rich hues of the stone – ranging from rust red and light brown to grey – add to the colourful scene.

The Ponta da Piedade: swarming with seagulls and boat trippers

Wild Scenery with Civilisation Round the Corner

The coastal rocks provide a habitat for numerous sea-birds, and agave plants cling for dear life on the edge of sheer drops high over the sea. Although the scenery is wild and natural, civilisation is never far away – you can't fail to miss the boxy concrete buildings above the small beaches north of the Ponta da Piedade, for example. A fun fact: the smallest beach here is called the Praia Grande ("Big Beach"). It's joined by more and more **beaches** as you head towards Lagos, including the Praia do Camilo, the Praia de Dona Ana and the Praia do Pinhão. If your boat moves away from the rock formations, you'll be able to see the holiday resort of Luz to the west and the mountains of the Serra de Monchique inland.

Boat trips are a really fantastic experience and a great way to fill up your cameras' memory cards! Don't fall into the trap of thinking you'll have the scenery all to yourself, however – the Ponta da Piedade is one of the region's

Western Algarve

truly unmissable highlights, and is filled with streams of visitors as a result. 🚼 Boat tours are also ideal for families with kids.

A landscape of changing light: boat tours along the rocky coast

TAKING A BREAK

When you're back on dry land, you might like to get some refreshments in the area around Lagos marina – opt for a cooling drink or a more opulent meal.

➕ 199 D2

INSIDER INFO

Insider Tip

- If possible, take a **boat trip** that starts from Lagos marina (▶ 132) instead of the nearer Praia de Dona Ana. Apart from increasing the sense of anticipation, the extra distance of the tours from the marina lets you sail past the mouth of the Bensafrim river and catch a glimpse of a small fort before making your slow approach to the rock formations of the Ponta da Piedade. You'll also get the best angles for photographing the masts in the marina on the outward and return journeys.
- **Cave tours** are better at low tide, when the boats have better access to the caverns. Seafaris (www.seafaris.net; tel. 282 798 727) offer reliable tours from €10 per person.
- Guided **sea kayak trips** offered by such organisations as the Kayak Centre (http://kayak-centre.com, tel. 917 691 761) start southwest of Lagos at the Praia do Porto de Mos. These tours usually last three hours and cost €25 per person.
- If in doubt, don't take a camera with you on a sea kayak trip. If you're inexperienced, it's easy to lose your balance and tip right over into the drink.
- Whatever you do, don't forget your **sun screen** on boat and kayak trips, even on cloudy days. The strength of the sun's rays out on the water is immense.

Insider Tip

- Head nearer the Ponta da Piedade to find some tiny **beaches** that can be reached via stairways (e.g. the Praia do Camilo and the Praia de Dona Ana).
- Walkers who dare to venture out onto the rocky outcrops above the Ponta da Piedade must be **extremely careful** indeed.

⭐ Cabo de São Vicente

The Cape of St. Vincent is Portugal's non plus ultra – the end of the world. It's also one of the most beautiful coastal headlands in Europe. The lighthouse can be seen rising above the rock for miles around, and the Atlantic views and oceanic atmosphere are terrific. The Cape's raw natural surroundings also attract numerous seabirds that come to nest or stop off on their journey further south.

The route from Sagres (➤ 146) to the Cabo de São Vicente gets more dramatic the further you go. It leads through a wild, hostile, scarcely populated area filled with low vegetation that's ravaged by a hellish wind. It's easy to find your way – just head towards the **lighthouse on the Cape**, which stands like a watchman in the landscape. The small road ends at a car park just before the headland where you'll find snack and souvenir stands that look out-of-place in the raw natural scene. Watch out when opening your car door – the wind can be strong enough to rip it out of your hands. The Cape also has some totally calm days, but they're the exception rather than the rule.

Come Face to Face with the Wild Atlantic

With its panoramic views and cliffs that plummet up to 230ft (70m) into the sea below, the landscape at the Cape is pretty hard to beat. The wind carries up the sound of the waves as they crash against the rocks, adding to the apocalyptic atmosphere. Nature fans who don't mind the elements will enjoy staying here for a long time and gazing out at the mounting waves and the dramatic lights on the horizon. The views northwards along the Costa Vicentina are particularly beautiful – the Atlantic seems to boil, foam and thunder with particular ferocity there.

Rounding the Cabo de São Vicente was seen as a challenge during the time of the Crusades

Southeast of the Cape you'll spot the relatively sheltered **Ensenada do Beliche**, a bay that stretches over to the **Ponta de Sagres** (➤ 128). If you want to escape the wind, take refuge in the lighthouse courtyard and the small museum.

Europe's Southwesternmost Tip

① **Cabo de São Vicente:** A fort with a monastery and accommodation for pilgrims was built here in the 16th century. It was destroyed in an attack by Sir Francis Drake in 1587. Today's fortress complex was built in the mid-19th century.

② **Lighthouse:** The Cabo de São Vicente is topped with a 22m (72ft)-high lighthouse (► 131).

③ **Ponta de Sagres:** The Ponta de Sagres is home to the Igreja de Nossa Senhora da Graça – a little church that dates back to the 16th century – and a few sparse remains of a former fortress.

The lighthouse on the Cape is real draw for sightseers and hikers alike

Cabo de São Vicente

The Ponta de Sagres and the Cabo de São Vicente combine to form the southwesternmost tip of Europe. This exposed cape was described 500 years ago by Luís de Camões, Portugal's national poet, as a place "where the land ends and the sea begins". Pliny the Elder also wrote that the Romans regarded the Cape and the nearby Ponta de Sagres as an ancient seat of the gods.

4 Fortaleza de Sagres: According to a controversial legend, geographers, astronomers and seafarers from several countries came to pool their knowledge in the fort on the Ponta de Sagres under the leadership of Henry the Navigator (▶ 16, 146). No trace remains of this 15th/16th-century seafaring academy, however. Today's fortress dates from 1793.

5 rosa dos ventos: This circle with a diameter of 43m (140ft) dates from the 15th century. Divided into 40 segments, it's popularly known as the "Rosa dos Ventos" (wind/compass rose). Its significance remains unclear.

A sundial or a navigational aid? The significance of the "windrose" in the Fortaleza de Sagres remains a mystery

Western Algarve

A Cape Steeped in Legend

Myths, legends and fragments of history surround the
Cabo de São Vicente. Prehistoric people – the very same
folk who built the dolmens that still stand near Vila do
Bispo and Raposeira today – were in awe of the Cape.
Along with the nearby Ponta de Sagres (▶ 128), it was
worshipped and venerated in ancient times as a holy
headland and a seat of the gods, perhaps inspired by
the wildness of the landscape itself. Whether the Romans
were referring to the Cape or the Ponta de Sagres when
they wrote about the *promontorium sacrum* high above
the Atlantic remains a mystery. It's thought that a
sanctuary or some kind of open-air temple was built on
the headland, although this remains unproven, as does
speculation that Saturn or Hercules were once venerated
here. The oldest record of the Cape comes from the Latin
poet Avienus, who mentioned the windswept promontory
in his *Ora maritima*, written in the 4th century AD.

Guarded by Ravens – the Relics of Saint Vincent

The Cape was given its current moniker – "São Vicente" –
much later on. The name refers to St Vincent, who was
martyred in Valencia in the early 4th century. According
to a popular version of his legend, the saint's body was
sewn into a sailor's kitbag, weighed down with stones and
sunk to the bottom of the sea. Despite these efforts to get
rid of him, his body drifted back to shore, where it was
discovered by two ravens that guarded Vincent's remains
from the other birds and animals. The corpse was later
discovered and given a burial by some religious passers-by.

INSIDER INFO

- Whatever you do, don't underestimate the powerful winds and the impassable **cliff
  landscape** around the Cabo de São Vicente. Under no circumstance should you dare
  to venture too close to the edge of the cliffs for a souvenir photo or a selfie. It's
  caused people to fall to their deaths before today.
- The Cape's small, rather modest **museum** (April–Sept, Tue–Sun 10am–6pm;
  rest of the year, Tue–Sun 10–5pm; entry €1.50) is more suited to people with a
  specialist interest in the model boats and nautical instruments etc. on display.

- Make sure to stop off at the car park above the **Praia do Beliche** on your trip to/from
  Sagres. This wonderful beach can't be seen from the road itself. A stairway leads
  down to the sand. The Praia do Beliche is popular with surfers and is sheltered
  from the strong north winds.
- You could also make another stop to see the remains of the **Fortress of Santa
  Catarina** on your way between Sagres and the Cabo de São Vicente.
- You won't find any tangible signs of the legend surrounding St Vincent on the Cabo
  de São Vicente. There's no longer a church on the Cape (if one ever existed here at
  all), and the Saint's remains have been worshipped in Lisbon since the late Middle
  Ages. Nevertheless, you'll still find a reliquary with a tiny piece of his bone in the
  equally tiny museum at **Vila do Bispo's parish church** nearby. Open at irregular hours,
  it's located about 15km (9mi) inland (northeast of the Cape).

The signal from the lighthouse on the south-westernmost point of the Iberian peninsula can be seen by ships 50km (31mi) away

After the Moorish invasion in the 8th century, Vincent had to be brought to safety to save him from potential desecration. A ship accompanied by ravens carried him from southern Spain up to the Cabo de São Vicente, where his relics were deposited in a small church that was already a well-known place of Christian pilgrimage. The birds stayed to keep watch over the building, which was named the Igreja do Corvo ("Church of the Raven") as a result. The relics were moved again to their final resting place in Lisbon in the 12th century. It's unclear how much of St Vincent's legend is based in truth. Whatever its provenance, however, the tale is inextricably intertwined with the story of the Cape, Portugal's "End of the World".

A Powerful Lighthouse

The story goes that a fortress, a lighthouse and a monastery were built on the site of the legendary "Church of the Raven". As well as defending this strategic position, it was the monks' job to keep the fire burning up on the lighthouse. The buildings were damaged again and again over the years due to earthquakes and attacks from enemy forces. The present lighthouse, surrounded by restored fortifications, dates from the year 1846 and was constructed during the reign of Dona Maria II. It has been updated with new lighting technology on a number of occasions – most recently at the start of this millennium. The squat building is topped with red and its light can be seen from over 50km (31 miles/27 nautical miles) away on a clear day.

TAKING A BREAK

You'll find stalls selling snacks at the car park by the Cabo de São Vicente. If you want something more substantial, head to Sagres or the small centre of Vila do Bispo.

Insider Tip

✚ 198 A1

㉛ Lagos

Lagos, the "Pearl of the Algarve", is an atmospheric town with 30,000 inhabitants and a great deal to offer: historic buildings, friendly streets and squares, a marina, and a promenade that runs along the final stretch of the Bensafrim river before it joins the Atlantic. It also has some small beaches and the Ponta da Piedade (► 124) on its doorstep. The Meia Praia, the longest beach with plenty of space to sunbathe, is found in the northeast of town.

Lagos has a long history. Its original name, *Lacobriga*, is thought to have Celtic origins, and the Phoenicians, Greeks, Romans and Moors have lived here down the centuries. Trade and the harbour have played an important role here since time immemorial. The late Middle Ages were a golden age for Lagos – the port served as a base for the ships that carried out the infamous **trade with Africa** and helped

A SAINT FROM LAGOS

Gonçalo de Lagos (1360–1422) is an established historical figure. Born in Lagos to a fisherman, it became apparent that he was a Christian at an early age. After his studies, he entered the Augustinian order and became the prior of several monasteries. He is said to have helped rescue a number of fishermen in a miraculous manner, a feat which cemented his saintly reputation.

Gonçalo de Lagos makes an appearance all over his hometown: you'll see a small likeness of him in the Arco de São Gonçalo (the city gate that bears his name), sculptures of him in the parish church of Santa Maria and the city museum, and a huge statue of him on the open space south of the small river fort of Ponta da Bandeira. Gonçalo de Lagos is believed to protect fishermen to this day.

Portugal become a great maritime power. Lagos was heavily involved in the Voyages of Discovery under **Prince Henry the Navigator** (1394–1460, ▶ 16) and became a transhipment point for precious exotic goods. Much to the shame of everyone involved, these "goods" also included slaves, who where treated like animals.

The first **slave market** took place here in 1444, thus opening a dark chapter in local history. The new-found wealth this commerce brought with it can be seen in the churches and houses of the era. Lagos became a playground for merchants, its walls were reinforced and new fortifications were built. The heavy earth and seaquake of 1755 was a setback, but Lagos was later revived by the fish canning industry, trading acumen and – last but not least – the rise of tourism. Lagos is one of the largest holiday destinations in the Algarve today.

Left: There are lots of atmospheric streets to explore in Lagos at night

Prestigious Squares and Baroque Magnificence

A popular starting point for a stroll through town is the **Praça Gil Eanes**, where you'll find a tourist information office, a strange modern sculpture in memory of King Sebastião (1554–1578) and the busy streets of the **pedestrian zone**. The Rua 25 de Abril is particularly lively and lined with numerous restaurants – it might be a good idea to book a table here for your evening meal.

The next important square is the **Praça do Infante Dom Henrique**, where you'll see the monument of Prince Henry the Navigator. A small arcade building in the square's northwest corner shows where the first slave market was held in 1444. Further structures here include the Baroque **Igreja de Santa Maria** (parish church), the former Governor's Palace (the seat of the Governors from the 14th century onwards), and a military warehouse from the 17th century that's emblazoned with a coat of arms.

The Igreja de Santa Maria and the slave market are lit up after dark

The **Igreja de Santo António** (18th century), Lagos' biggest cultural attraction, is tucked away on a site two streets further on from the Praça do Infante Dom Henrique. The interior of this Baroque church is abundantly decorated with azulejos, gilded wood carvings and paintings depicting scenes from the life of Saint Anthony. If you want to check out the interior of the sacred building, you'll have to pay to go through the **Museu Municipal Dr. José Formosinho** (the Municipal Museum). The museum's several small rooms contain archaeological findings, ceramics, model boats, paintings with images of the Algarve, a weapons collection, porcelain figurines, silver bowls, medals, coins and lace work. There's also a department dedicated to sacred art.

Fishing is a tradition that continues in Lagos and other parts of the Algarve to this day

Beaches and Fortress Walls

You'll spot the best-preserved part of the **town's walls to the** south of the Praça do Infante Dom Henrique. Palm trees provide some shade. There's also a monument to Gil Eanes, one of the most significant players in the Voyages of Discovery under Prince Henry the Navigator in the 15th century. Go a little further and you'll see the town's finest gate, the Arco de São Gonçalo (14th century). Cross the street to the small castello that's open to visitors. Called the **Forte Ponta da Bandeira**, it was built at the mouth of the river of Bensafrim to defend the old port at the end of the 17th century.

Insider Tip

Head south of the fortress to the small beaches that line the coast towards the Ponta da Piedade (▶ 124):

INSIDER INFO

A new tourist attraction at Lagos Marina is the **Museu de Cera dos Descobrimentos** (www.museuceradescobrimentos.com, daily 10am–6pm, €5), a wax museum that documents the Portuguese Age of Discoveries with models of such key figures as Prince Henry the Navigator and Vasco da Gama.

🛝 A VERY SPECIAL ZOO

Families with kids staying in Lagos might like to take a trip out to visit the Parque Zoológico de Lagos. Despite its name, it isn't in the city itself – it lies around 10km (6mi) to the northwest between Bensafrim and Barão de São João. The zoo is a rather special affair – visitors have the chance to get much closer than usual to a number of species, including flamingos. Birds chirrup and coo everywhere you go. An extensive lake area includes islands for monkeys and lemurs. Peacocks, geese and ducks strut around freely on the path. A separate pet section lets you and your offspring loose on enclosures filled with sheep, goats, ponies, rabbits and guinea pigs. The Parque Zoológico de Lagos (www. zoolagos.com) is open April–Sept, daily 10–7; Oct–Mar, daily 10–5; entry costs €16 for adults and €12 for kids (4–11 years). There's a restaurant by the entrance if you get peckish.

the Praia da Batata, the Praia dos Estudantes, the Praia do Pinhão, the Praia de Dona Ana, the Praia do Camilo and the Praia Grande. Some are only accessible via steep steps.

At 4km (2.5mi) in length, the **Meia Praia** – which borders the Ria de Alvor (► 145) to the east – is the longest beach in Lagos. It starts on the other side of the estuary, so you'll have to make a longer detour inland if you want to drive there: the route leads over railway tracks and through an extensive landscape of dunes. You'll spot a few hotels behind the beach itself.

Market and Marina

Further attractions worth checking out in Lagos are the market hall on the Avenida dos Descobrimentos and the marina (which can be reached via a pedestrian crossing). **Boat trips** to the Ponta da Piedade (► 124) and 🛝 dolphin watching tours set sail from the latter. There are good chances of seeing **dolphins** far out to sea.

If you need a change from the beach, make a trip inland to the Barragem da Bravura reservoir. The journey (around 15km/9mi) takes you via Odiáxere.

TAKING A BREAK

You'll find lots of places for refreshments between the Praça Gil Eanes and the Praça do Infante Dom Henrique, particularly along the Rua 25 de Abril. The marina is also a good option – take a seat on one of the many terraces and admire the yachts.

➕ 199 D2 📍 Largo Rossio de São João; connections to Albufeira, Armação de Pêra, Burgau, Cabo de São Vicente (seasonal), Faro, Lagoa, Portimão, Sagres, Vila do Bispo, etc.; www.eva-bus.com 🚉 Estrada de São Roque; connections to Faro, etc.; www.cp.pt

Posto de Turismo
✉ Praça Gil Eanes, Antigos Paços do Concelho ☎ 282 763 031; www.cm-lagos.pt 🕐 July–mid-Sept, daily 9–7; rest of year Mon–Sat 9:30–5:30

Igreja de Santo António/Museu Municipal Dr. José Formosinho
✉ Rua General Alberto da Silveira 🕐 Tue–Sun 10am–12:30, 2pm–5:30pm 🎟 €3

Forte Ponta da Bandeira
✉ Cais da Solaria 🕐 Tue–Sun 10–6 🎟 €3

㉜ Serra de Monchique

In terms of its landscape and climate, the Serra de Monchique is the polar opposite of the coastal Algarve. This mountain range in the vast hinterland behind Lagos and Portimão reaches a height of 902m (2,960ft). Crisscrossed by creeks, streams and lush greenery, it's the loftiest place in the region. A road leads up to Fóia, the summit that boasts some spectacular views.

When it's particularly hot on the coast, you might be very glad of a trip up to the cooler climes of the Serra de Monchique. The mountains are home to **over 1,000 species of plant** – the air is filled with the scent of eucalyptus and wild flowers; pines, cork oaks and sweet chestnut trees add a touch of greenery; and locals use the fruits of the strawberry tree to make *medronho*, a type of brandy with a kick. If you're

Stop off at the spa town of Caldas de Monchique that sits high up in the mountains

---

🚸 THE PARQUE DA MINA – FUN FOR ALL THE FAMILY

You'll spot the Parque da Mina (www.parquedamina.pt, April–Sept. daily 10–7; Oct–Mar, daily 10–5; Nov–Jan closed Monday; €10, Kids 4–11 €6) along the road that leads from Portimão to the Serra de Monchique. It was once home to a barite, copper and iron mine. Today, the site boasts extensive green grounds and is a good destination for families with children. As well as kids' play equipment and a bird enclosure, you'll find pens filled with ponies, donkeys and pot-bellied pigs. You can buy food for them at the entrance. Another tourist attraction at the park is the former mine owners' country house. It boasts a collection of wall clocks, grandfather clocks and musical instruments. The junction to the Parque da Mina (turn right) is signposted on the road from Portimão to Caldas de Monchique.

The view from Fóia, the highest point in the Algarve

feeling adventurous, the Serra is a great place for **walking**. The Via Algarviana trail cuts through the mountains, and Mount Picota is a popular place for hikes. Hardcore cyclists love powering up the road to Fóia. Getting here from the coast is easy: just head north on the N266, a highway that winds upwards via Caldas de Monchique and the village of Monchique.

A Spa in the Foothills

If you like spas, you'll love **Caldas de Monchique** in the foothills of the Serra. It's a good base for exploring the region, and has a few places to stay. The town's claim to fame is that it's the only spa resort in the Algarve. It lies in a lush, green valley a little way from the main road, about 20km (12mi) north of Portimão. The place is steeped in history – the healing waters were used in Roman times, and King João II stayed here in 1495. The Bishop of the Algarve had the first bathing house with a sick bay built in the town in the 1600s. Tourism got underway in 1899 with the opening of the Hotel Central. Extensive work has been carried out to bring the town's facilities up to modern standards. Nevertheless, it's still a down-to-earth place – if you want the last word in luxury, you'll have to look elsewhere. The waters, filled with bicarbonate, sodium and fluorine, are great for anyone suffering from respiratory, muscle, joint and bone issues. Spa guests and visitors gather on the central elm-lined promenade and in the small park that's filled with trees and water. People of a superstitious bent go there to drink from the "Fountain of Youth" and the "Source of Love". The town also has a small church – the Capela de Santa Teresa.

Insider Tip

The Capital of the Mountains

Monchique, the most important town in the mountains, was once known for its woodcarving and wool and linen weaving. The town and its sea of white houses climbing up the slopes look rather modest today. Check out the 15th/16th-century **Igreja Matriz** with its squat bell tower

and Manueline portal. The revered likeness of the Virgin Mary *(Nossa Senhora da Conceição)* inside the church is attributed to the sculptor Joaquim Machado de Castro (1731–1822). A short way above the village you'll find the remains of the Convento de Nossa Senhora do Desterro, a monastery that was founded in 1631 and heavily damaged by the earthquake of 1755. An 8km (5mi)-long stretch of road leads from Monchique up to **Fóia**, the highest point in the Algarve. You might be put off at first glance by the signs of modernity in the mountains – wind turbines have been set up in the hills, and Fóia itself is home to antenna masts and a large car park. Nevertheless, the views down to the Atlantic and the coastal foothills are absolutely spectacular! *Insider Tip*

The people in the mountains eat heartier meals than their compatriots on the coast, but never fear – you can still find salad and seafood in the Serra!

TAKING A BREAK

The main square in Monchique is a popular, peaceful place for a drink and a bite to eat. You'll also find some roadside restaurants as you drive up to Fóia.

➕ 199 E5 🚌 Connections to Portimão; www.frotazul-algarve.pt

Posto de Turismo
✉ Largo de S. Sebastião, Monchique
☎ 282 911 189; www.cm-monchique.pt
🕐 Mon–Fri 9:30am–1pm, 2pm–5:30pm

INSIDER INFO

- Try a sip of clear "medronho" (a brandy made from the fruit of the strawberry tree) and taste some hearty game dishes and sausages while you're in the Serra de Monchique. They also make some exceptional **honey** *(mel)* here – the region has been known for producing and selling it for centuries.
- Don't play with fire in the mountains. There's a big **risk of forest fires**!
- Such companies as Monchique Passeios na Serra offer guided **walking tours** in the mountains (tel. 962 543 217, http://passeiosnaserra.com/en, info@passeiosnaserra.com; prices start at €15 per person for a group of ten people; €30 per person for a group of four). The walks include a chance to test out some tasty treats from the region.
- *Insider Tip* It's safe to drink fresh **spring water** in the mountains. Locals use springs to fill their water cans and bottles as they head up to Fóia from Monchique.
- *Insider Tip* Take the route that travels via Alferce on your way up or down – you'll be able to make a short detour to the **Barragem de Odelouca** reservoir (► 176).

At Your Leisure

33 Armação de Pêra

This former fishing village at the mouth of the Ribeira de Alcantarilha has grown into a small holiday resort. Tuna and sardines used to be caught and salted here before being sold to other parts of the country. The memory of this trade – which still carries on to a certain extent today – lives on in the name of the town's beach, the Praia dos Pescadores ("Fishermen's Beach"). A fortress was built here in the 17th century, although it has all but disappeared over the course of time. The major tourist money-spinner and the main reason to visit Armação de Pêra is the **Praia Grande**, the long beach southeast of the heavily developed little town. The beach boasts beautiful expanses of sand bordered by dunes. As elsewhere, wooden walkways have been set up to protect the dunes and provide a path to the beach.

The **Lagoa dos Salgados** – a lagoon that's reached via a track – stretches out behind the dunes that line the Praia Grande. The route there isn't well signposted. The lagoon is a hotspot for birdwatchers. *Insider Tip* Depending on the time of day and the season (and with a bit of luck and a lot of patience!), you might get to see some flamingos. You're more likely to spy herons, coots, ferruginous ducks and western swamp hens. 🚻 Families with nature-loving kids will enjoy it, too. There's a special atmosphere round the lake in the evening – the building developments in the background are only a minor disturbance. The Lagoa dos Salgados, one of the Algarve's most beautiful bodies of water, occasionally makes the

🚻 SAND SCULPTURE FESTIVAL

The *Festival Internacional de Escultura em Areia* – the International Sand Sculpture Festival that's known as the "*Fiesa*" for short – takes place every year between Pêra and Algoz from around mid/late March to mid/late October. Participants from all over the world make the journey here to create fantastic sculptures with innumerable tonnes of sand. The festival has a different theme every year and is a popular attraction for families with kids. Entry costs €9 for adults and €4.50 for kids aged 6–12. Visit the festival's website (www.fiesa.org) to find out more information.

headlines because it's being threatened by yet another proposed construction project. Let's hope they never come to fruition.

Armação de Pêra isn't exactly a coastal beauty, but the promenade is tolerable. The small town's population increases many times over during the summer months, and it's a good base for exploring the beaches and sandy bays in the surrounding area. If you head to the southeast, you'll find the famously beautiful **Praia da Galé**. Travel west, and you'll come across the **Praia da Cova Redonda**, the **Praia dos**

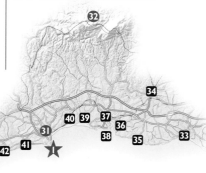

Western Algarve

👫 EXPENSIVE PLEASURES

The zoo, theme park and aqua park near Guia on the N125 will stretch your holiday budget somewhat (www.zoomarine.pt, Mar–Oct; entry times change depending on the season, 10am–5/6/7:30pm; June–August open every day, otherwise closed on some days, see the calendar on the website; €29, kids up to 10, €19). The Slide & Splash aquapark (www.slidesplash.com, €26, kids aged 5–10, €19) by Estômbar is open from April to October. Aqualand Algarve, another water park near Alcantarilha, is open between mid-June and early September (http://www.aqualand.pt, €22.50, kids aged 5–10, €16.50, cheaper deals available online). You may be glad to hear you don't usually have to pay an entrance fee for very small children. It can also be worth buying a family ticket if they're available when you're planning to go.

34 Silves

Silves boasts orange groves, the Rio Arade and its striking twin monuments up on the hill: the **Sé Velha** – the "old cathedral" which originates from the 13th–15th century and was supposedly built on the site of a former mosque – and the mighty, crenelated **castelo** (castle) that brings the Algarve's Moorish past to life more vividly than any other building in the region. Silves emerged as a Moorish stronghold in the 700s and became the capital of the Algarve in the 11th century. In its heyday, it was said to have surpassed Lisbon in terms of its size and importance. Silves served as a centre of flourishing Islamic culture, poetry and thought until it was conquered by Christian troops in the 13th century. Silves' importance later began to decline – the Arade river, once a vital waterway, silted up, and trade with North Africa came to a close. The bishopric of Silves was moved to Faro in the 16th century. The cork industry breathed new

Beijinhos and the **Praia da Senhora da Rocha**. The white, stocky **Ermida de Nossa Senhora da Rocha** – one of the region's pilgrimage chapels dedicated to the Virgin Mary – sits above the Praia da Senhora da Rocha. Visitors can examine the sculpture of the Mother and Child (which dates from the 16th century) more closely through a large pane of glass. You can also admire some beautiful views from the narrow cliff-top outcrop that juts out over the Atlantic.

✚ 200 C2

Posto de Turismo

✉ Avenida Marginal, Armação de Pêra

☎ 282 312 145

life into Silves in the 19th century. Now home to 11,000 inhabitants, the town is a popular inland tourist destination today. It only takes half a day to explore.

Covering an area of 12,000m² (130,000ft²), the mighty fortress was the largest in the Algarve during the Middle Ages. Its Muslim builders are thought to have reused material from a previous late-Roman or Visigoth structure. The castle has undergone extensive renovation work, and some parts of it look out-of-place and not in-keeping with the original style as a result. Nevertheless, it's still interesting to walk among its walls and watch-towers. Inside the complex you'll find an open square and an outlet that leads to a cistern that's known locally as the "Cistern of the Enchanted Moorish Woman".

Traces of Silves' eventful past can also be found in the **Casa da Cultura Islâmica e Mediterrânica** (House of Islamic and Mediterranean culture) and the **Museu Municipal de Arqueologia** (Municipal Archaeology Museum), which boasts a fountain of Islamic origin. It's also worth heading to the lower part of town and taking a stroll along the **esplanade** with its water features and modern sculptures. Musical events are occasionally held there.

200 B3 buses to Albufeira and Armação de Pêra, etc.

Posto de Turismo
Estrada Nacional 124, Silves
282 442 255 Mon–Fri 9:30–1, 2–6

FESTIVALS

A fixed date in Lagos' festival calendar is the historical *Festival dos Descobrimentos* (Festival of Discoveries) in late April/early May. The *Feira do Presunto* ("Festival of Ham") and the *Festival do Medronho* ("Festival of Strawberry Tree Brandy") are held in Monchique at the end of July. Silves plays host to a large medieval festival, the *Feira Medieval*, around the middle of August. It boasts over a week's worth of events. Also around mid-August is the *Festival da Sardinha*, a large sardine festival that's held on the riverbank in Portimão. If you're in the Algarve in October, you can also attend the *Festival de Observação de Aves*, the bird-watching festival in Sagres.

The cathedral and the castle both rise above the roofs of Silves

Castelo
Daily; mid-June to end of Sept, 9–7; Oct–mid-June, 9–5:30 €2.80, Combiticket with the Museu Municipal de Arqueologia €3.90

Museu Municipal de Arqueologia
Rua da Porta de Loulé 14
Daily 10am–6pm
€2.10, Combiticket with the castelo €3.90

Casa da Cultura Islâmica e Mediterrânica
Largo da República, Jardim Cancela de Abreu Free

Sé Velha
Mon–Sat 9am–1pm and Mon–Fri 2pm–6pm
€1

35 Carvoeiro

It might be small, but Carvoeiro is a firm tourist favourite in the western Algarve. This former fishing village has blossomed into a town of 3,000 inhabitants that stretches a little way inland and boasts plenty of restaurants and bars. The highlights are the small promenade and the Praia do Carvoeiro, the **main beach** that's bordered by cliffs. Fishermen still pull their boats up onto the sand. For a touch of paradise, head to the Praia do Paraíso in the west of town. **Boat tours** are available along the rugged coast that's lined with natural caves, rock formations

Picturesque in the evening light: Ferragudo on the Rio Arade

and crevices in the stone. If you'd rather keep your feet on dry land, stroll along one **Insider Tip** of the **walkways** that start up on the hills behind the modern church of Nossa Senhora da Encarnação and lead eastwards along the cliffs to Algar Seco (about ten minutes' walk). There are some great sea views along the way. You'll end up at a car park. Head down the steps to find a restaurant and a vantage point and feast your eyes on the rock formations. Further inland, agave plants dominate the scene. Travel a short way east to find some more **beaches**. The first you'll come across is the Praia de Vale Covo. If you keep going towards Armação de Pêra, you'll discover the Praia do Carvalho, the Praia de Benagil and the particularly idyllic Praia da Marinha.

➕ 200 B2

Posto de Turismo
✉ Praia do Carvoeiro
☎ 282 357 728; www.carvoeiro.com

🗿 Ferragudo

Ferragudo – home to 2,000 people and located on the eastern side of the Rio Arade estuary – looks at once lovely and a little bit... odd.

It's lovely because it's retained the feel of a fishing village in its centre and along the river, and because there's lots to see and do around the **village square** – the Plaça Rainha Dona Leonor. It's also little odd, however, because of the rather unbeautiful sea of houses in Portimão and Praia da Rocha on the opposite side of the Rio Arade. Don't worry, though – this won't ruin your visit!

You won't see any signs of mass tourism in Ferragudo. Stroll along the river bank and admire the fishing boats and stacks of fish traps you'll find there. Pay a visit to the art exhibitions organised by the **Arte Algarve** art association. The beaches are also a pleas- **Insider Tip** ant surprise. Visitors are spoilt for choice with the **Praia Grande**, the **Praia do Pintadinho** (which sits beneath a modern concrete lighthouse), and the Praia do Molhe (which lies next to a breakwater in the Arade estuary). Head towards Carvoeiro to reach the last beach, the **Praia dos Caneiros**.

Walk to the upper part of Ferragudo to see the church (the **Igreja de Nossa Senhora da Conceição**) and a *miradouro* (vantage point). The Castelo de

São João Arade – a little castle that's set a short way away from the rest of the village – once helped the fort of Santa Catarina protect the estuary. It's an eye-catching sight, but isn't open to visitors.

➕ 200 A2

Galeria Arte Algarve
✉ Rua 25 de Abril 55–57 ☎ 282 425 082; www.artealgarve.net 🕐 Tue–Sat 11am–9pm

🖸 Portimão

The long history and medieval character of Portimão – a town of 50,000 inhabitants that sits next to the Rio Arade – have sadly been lost in the depths of time. Architectural developments have made large parts of it rather un-sightly and chaotic. Nevertheless, there are some highlights to focus on: the pleasant **riverside zone** with its marina and abundance of places to sit (follow signs to the *Zona Ribeirinha*) and the interesting **Museu de Portimão**. Housed in a converted fish cannery, this modern museum is truly unique. Its permanent exhibition, entitled "Territory and Identity", deals with such subjects as fishing and fish processing. Film recordings and sound effects make for a lively visit. The exhibits include machines employed in canning fish and old tools used for building boats. The displays also include some artefacts from the Roman era, including *amphorae* for the transportation of fish products and oil. A staircase that's somewhat tucked away in a corner leads down to an inter-esting water cistern. Part of the building is dedicated to special exhibitions. Unusually, the museum has later opening hours in August. Admission is free from 10am–2pm on Saturdays and all day on three special dates every

Insider Tip

year. See the website for more details.

Boat tours down the Rio Arade also leave from Portimão. It was once possible to navigate deep into the region's interior down this river, which served as a trade route for the Phoenicians, Greeks, Romans and Moors.

➕ 200 A3
🚌 Largo do Dique; connections to Albufeira, Armação de Pêra, Carvoeiro, Faro, Lagos, Loulé, Sagres, Vila do Bispo, etc.; www.eva-bus.com

Posto de Turismo
✉ Edifício Tempo/Teatro Municipal, Largo 1° de Dezembro
☎ 282 402 487; http://visitportimao.com
🕐 Mon–Fri 9:30am–6:30pm, Sat 10am–1pm, 2pm–6:30pm (subject to change)

Museu de Portimão
✉ Rua D. Carlos I.
☎ 282 405 230; www.museudeportimao.pt
🕐 Sept–Jul, Tue 2:30pm–6pm, Wed–Sun 10am–6pm; Aug, Tue 7:30pm–11pm, Wed–Sun 3pm–11pm 🎟 €3

🖸 Praia da Rocha

This suburb to the south of Portimão knows how to live the high life in summer. Visitors come here for a reason, and peace and quiet definitely isn't on their agenda. Praia da Rocha borders the **Rio Arade** estuary and boasts some **spotless white sandy beaches** that can be accessed from the upper part of town.

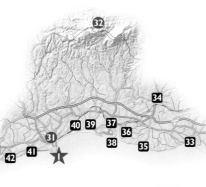

Western Algarve

This beach resort was discovered by tourists in the late 1800s. At first, wealthy families from southern Portugal and Spain were the only ones to visit. Before long, however, tourists began to flock in from all over the world.

As so often happened back then, this gave rise to a number of architectural eyesores. The faceless buildings above the beach are certainly not to everyone's taste.

Walkways run through the sand at the eastern part of the beach, making it easier to get to the restaurants. The **Fortaleza de Santa Catarina** – a small fortress complex built in the 1600s to protect the mouth of the river – provides an oasis of calm away from the hustle and bustle in the upper part of the suburb. It boasts some beautiful views of the marina and else-where. Rock formations dominate the scene, as do the 🛝 well-loved, picturesque beaches further west towards Alvor, such as the **Praia do Vau**, the **Praia da Prainha** and the **Praia dos Três Irmãos** (all popular destinations for families with kids).
✚ 200 A2

Posto de Turismo
✉ Avenida Tomás Cabreira ☎ 282 419 132

39 Alvor

Life goes on at its usual, provincial pace in the **Old Town district** of Alvor. It sits up on a hill, and surrounds the remains of a tiny medieval castle, the market and the **Igreja Matriz** parish church (16th century). The streets are narrow. Some of the houses have laundry outside and are covered in azulejos with geometric floral patterns. It might look modest at first glance, but give it a chance – the location makes some parts of Alvor extremely attractive.

The town abuts the Ria de Alvor (➤ 145) to the west, where you'll find the *Zona Ribeirinha* ("riverside zone") with its restaurants and harbour. It also meets the Praia de Alvor to the south. This wonderful, sandy beach stretches down to the mouth of the Ria de Alvor and merges into the Praia da Torralta to the east. Some ugly concrete blocks have been built by the sand, but

The parish church is the absolute jewel in Alvor's crown

they won't spoil your enjoyment of the beach itself. It's great to stroll along the walkways in the dunes behind the Praia de Alvor. They go down to the **Ria de Alvor** (►below).

There has been a settlement in and around Alvor since prehistoric times. This becomes particularly clear if you make a detour inland to the **Alcalar Monumentos Megalíticos**, a small site of restored megaliths. Located around 8km (5mi) north of Alvor, the stones date from the 3rd millennium BC.

➕ 199 E2

Posto de Turismo
✉ Rua Dr. Afonso Costa 51 ☎ 282 457 540

Alcalar Monumentos Megalíticos
✉ Take the signed junction off the N125
☎ 282 471 410; www.monumentosdoalgarve.pt
🕐 Sept–Jul, Tue–Sat 10am–1pm, 2pm–4:30pm; Aug, Tue–Sat 10am–1pm, 2pm–6pm 💷 €2

40 Ria de Alvor

Salt and fresh water merge in the Ria de Alvor, a waterway which scoops up several small rivers from the **Serra de Monchique** (►136) and funnels them all into the Atlantic. The estuary meets the Meia Praia, the beach at **Lagos** (►132), to the west and the Praia de Alvor, the beach at **Alvor** (►144), to the east. The Ria de Alvor has great ecological significance and is one of the best waterways for bird-watching in the Algarve.

Oystercatchers and sandwich terns can be seen here alongside black-winged stilts, curlew sandpipers, Kentish plover, seagulls and flamingos. You'll see local cocklepickers at work in the marshy landscape at low tide. The mud glistens in the sun, and the tang of salt hangs in the air.

🚶 Well-built walking trails run near the banks of the Ria de Alvor. They start on the Alvor side (to the southwest of the harbour) and stretch across to the dunes at the Praia de Alvor and the stone wall at the outlet of the river. This lengthy network of trails is also suitable for families with kids. Bird fans should bring binoculars, but it's worth having a walk through these natural surroundings even if you're not interested in our feathered friends. Regular seasonal boat tours set off from Alvor's *Zona Ribeirinha* ("riverside zone"), where you can get good refreshments and enjoy views of the river.

➕ 199 E2

Alvor Boat Trips
✉ Zona Ribeirinha, Alvor
☎ 966 807 621; www.alvorboattrips.com
🕐 Launch times depend on the tides
💷 one-hour boat tour €15

41 Luz

This **beach and holiday resort** in the western part of the municipality of Lagos isn't a stronghold of mass produced, cookie-cutter tourism – it's managed to keep its friendly atmosphere. This is thanks to its inhabitants, its small restaurants, its little places to stay, its promenade lined with palm trees and lanterns, and its beautiful sandy beach. The Igreja Matriz, a church recognisable from its chunky tower, houses an altarpiece from the 18th century. The former fortress is home to a restaurant today. The Carthaginians and Romans once lived here and produced salted fish. A Roman burial site has been found in nearby Cerro de Lorvão.

➕ 199 D2

42 Burgau

The whitewashed **coastal village** of Burgau sits high above the sea a little further to the west of Luz, its slightly larger neighbour. Places like Burgau and Luz have managed to resist the grip of mass tourism and stand out thanks to their friendly character and small eateries. The **beach**, bordered by mighty rocks, is as nice as the village itself.

Insider Tip

BEACHES TO THE WEST OF BURGAU

If you're feeling adventurous and have a car, head out west from Burgau to discover such beautiful, wildly romantic beaches as the **Praia de Cabanas Velhas**, the **Praia da Boca do Rio** and the **Praia da Salema**. The village of Salema itself is a good spot for a short break along the way. Afterwards, you might like to extend your day trip with a detour to the isolated **Praia das Furnas** (a difficult drive; there are interesting natural stone arches on the beach), and to the equally worthwhile **Praia do Zavial** (with a restaurant at the entrance). Bear in mind that the wide sandy beaches can be swallowed up at high tide. Make a loop inland on the return journey. If you drive a short way along the N125, you'll get the chance to make a cultural stop at the **Ermida de Nossa Senhora de Guadalupe** (May–Sept, Tue–Sun 10:30am–1pm, 2pm–6:30pm; Oct–Apr, Tue–Sun 9:30am–1pm and 2pm–5pm). Prince Henry the Navigator (➤ 16) is said to have attended mass often at this lonely chapel in the 15th century.

Burgau once belonged to a network of coastal fortifications built in the 16th/17th century (along with Boca do Rio, Figueira, Luz, Zavial, Baleeira and Beliche).
➕ 198 C2

43 Sagres

Sagres deserves to be seen as more than just a stop-off point on the road to the legendary **Cabo de São Vicente** (➤ 127). The town shouldn't be judged by its sober entrance or some of its disappointing streets – it's got so much more to offer than that! Take the exceptionally picturesque **fishing harbour**, for example, where – if you come at the right time – you can watch fishermen unloading the fresh catch of the day. Head a little further northeast to find a protected stretch of coastline that boasts the sandy **Praia do Martinhal** and, further south, the wild landscape around the **Ponta de Sagres** (➤ 128). This cliff-lined headland was venerated as a sacred spot back in pre-Roman times. Part of the rugged promontory is taken up by the **Fortaleza**, a fortress with medieval origins that's been given national monument status. Although not much remains of the original building, and despite the jarring modern structures that have been added to the complex, it's still a place that's steeped in history. It was here that Prince Henry the Navigator (1394–1460) was said to have founded the nautical school of Sagres, thus laying the foundations for Portugal's seafaring prowess. Although many researchers regard this as a total myth, it is known for sure that Prince Henry did come here to found the settlement known as Vila do Infante. He died in Sagres in November 1460. The "wind rose" and chapel are interesting highlights of the fortress. You should also spend some time strolling around the network of paths on the Ponta de Sagres and enjoying the magnificent views across to the Cabo de São Vicente. A further beach, the **Praia do Tonel**, lies west of the Ponta de Sagres. You'll find some accommodation and a number of family-run restaurants in Sagres itself. The town is also a popular base for surfers.
➕ 198 C2
🚌 Buses to Lagos, Vila do Bispo and the Cabo de São Vicente (seasonal), etc.

Posto de Turismo
✉ Avenida Comandante Matoso ☎ 282 624 873
🕐 Tue–Sat 9am–12:30 & 1:30pm–5:30pm

Fortaleza de Sagres
✉ Ponta de Sagres
☎ 282 620 142; www.monumentosdoalgarve.pt
🕐 Daily; July, Aug 9:30am–8:30pm; May, Jun, Sept 9:30am–8pm; April, Oct 9:30am–6:30pm; Nov–Mar 9:30am–5:30pm 🎫 €3

Where to...
Stay

Prices
for a double room per night in the high season
€ under 90 euros   €€ 90–150 euros   €€€ over 150 euros

ALPORCHINHOS

Vilalara Thalassa Resort €€€
This top-class resort on a lush, 11ha (27 acre) site to the west of Armação de Pêra offers stunning sea views and all the amenities you'd expect from a spa hotel. The cuisine is exquisite. A large thalassotherapy (seawater) program is designed to bring harmony to your body and mind.
✚ 200 C2
✉ Praia das Gaivotas, Alporchinhos
☎ 282 320 000; www.vilalararesort.com

CARVOEIRO

Casa Luiz €
This accommodation in the upper part of Carvoeiro is close enough to the holiday crowds to be practical, but far enough away to be peaceful. Guests can choose between two spacious rooms, a studio and an apartment. It's only a few minutes' walk to the main beach and even closer to the pretty walkway that starts behind the small church of Nossa Senhora da Encarnação and heads to Algar Seco. The weekly rates are very attractive in winter. **Insider Tip**
✚ 200 B2
✉ Rampa Nossa Senhora da Encarnação 5
☎ 282 354 058; www.casaluiz.com

FERRAGUDO

Hotel Casabela €€€
This four-star hotel lies outside Ferragudo, away from the centre of mainstream tourism. It stands out thanks to its beautiful sea views (which are reflected in the price). The pool is quite small, but it isn't very far to the nearest beach. It's usually only open from February to November.
✚ 200 A2
✉ Vale de Areia, Ferragudo
☎ 282 490 650; www.hotel-casabela.com

LAGOS

Marina Club Lagos Resort €€€
Visitors can choose between studios and suites in this appealing complex behind the marina. Its location means you're close enough to all the action without getting smothered by it. The facilities include a central pool, a spa, the Regata Club Bar and the Way Point restaurant. The Old Town is easily accessible on foot. They offer some attractive prices during the low season!
✚ 199 D2 ✉ Marina de Lagos
☎ 282 790 600; www.marinaclub.pt

Marina Rio €€
Accommodation with great service that's often praised in all the right online forums. It's separated from the marina by a road. You can reach the Old Town on foot in about ten minutes.
✚ 199 D2 ✉ Avenida dos Descobrimentos
☎ 282 780 830; www.marinario.com

Vila Galé Lagos €€€
A beautiful hotel complex in the eastern part of town. It's set in generous grounds about 400m behind the Meia Praia. There's an

impressively landscaped outdoor pool, two tennis courts, an indoor pool, a sauna and a fitness room. It's cheaper in the low season!

➕ 199 D2
✉ Rua Sophia de Melo Breyner Andresen
☎ 282 771 400; www.vilagale.com

LUZ

Luz Beach Apartments €–€€

These apartments right behind the beach in the holiday resort of Luz are a good choice for independent holidaymakers. 👪 Families with kids will also appreciate them – the facilities and pricing structure (with the option of an extra bed) are tailored to their needs. The minimum stay is four nights during the high season (and three nights at other times of the year).

➕ 199 D2
✉ Rua do Poço, Praia da Luz
☎ 282 792 677; www.luzbeachapartments.com

RAPOSEIRA

Good Feeling €

If you're searching for a low-cost hotel in the far west of the region, then look no further than this place in Raposeira, a village located half way between Lagos and the Cabo de São Vicente. Run by Miguel and Hugo, two Portuguese friends, the hostel is popular with surfers and young people. You'll get to meet other travellers in the communal kitchen, the living room or out on the terrace. Guests can choose between double and shared rooms. The private studio is slightly more expensive (€–€€).

➕ 198 B2 ✉ Sítio Eiras de Cima, Raposeira
☎ 914 658 807; www.thegoodfeeling.com

SAGRES

Baleeira €€–€€€

Four-star comfort off the beaten track. It's located a little way above Sagres harbour. The design is con-temporary. The facilities include a pool, spa, restaurant, bar and lounge. Sports fans can also book surfing courses. Prices vary enormously.

➕ 198 B1
✉ Sítio da Baleeira
☎ 282 624 212; www.memmohotels.com

👪 Martinhal Beach Resort & Hotel €€€

This luxurious resort that's designed to look like a village is geared to families with kids and offers pools, sports and other activities. Located outside Sagres, it boasts a nice view back to town. The outdoor areas are spacious, and there's a direct route to Praia do Martinhal beach. Several restaurants and a spa.

➕ 198 B1
✉ Quinta do Martinhal, Apartado 54
☎ 282 240 200; www.martinhal.com

SERRA DE MONCHIQUE

Villa Termal das Caldas de Monchique Spa Resort €€–€€€

There are five places to stay in this spa town. The Hotel Central has retained all its late-19th-century charm. The D. Lourenço guest house (estalagem) sits right next to the elm-lined promenade. The Hotel D. Carlos looks like a large villa and offers beautiful, lush green views from its balconies. The Hotel Termal with its rather faceless, block-like architecture is integrated into the spa complex itself. Finally, there's the small, somewhat more expensive D. Francisco apartment complex. Its spa facilities and swimming pools (indoor/outdoor) are relatively small. The atmosphere is casual throughout. Lower prices are offered during the off season. Keep your eyes peeled for attractive fixed-priced package deals that include accommodation, food and use of the spa facilities.

➕ 199 E4 ✉ Caldas de Monchique
☎ 282 910 910; www.monchiquetermas.com

Where to...
Eat and Drink

Prices
for a three-course set menu without drinks or service
€ under 20 euros   €€ 20–35 euros   €€€ over 35 euros

ALGAR SECO

Bistrobar Algar Seco €
An ideal place for drinks, refreshments and light meals. It can be reached by strolling along the walkway that leads to Algar Seco from the church of Nossa Senhora da Encarnação in the upper part of Carvoeiro.
➕ 200 B2
✉ Rua das Flores, Algar Seco
☎ 282 350 449; www.algarseco.pt/bistrobar.htm
🕐 Daily 9:30am–9pm
(Lunch noon–3:30pm, Dinner 5:30pm–9pm)

ALVOR

O Luís €€–€€€
This beach restaurant in a fantastic location gives you the opportunity to flame your own steak at the table and taste some delicious seafood while you gaze out at the waves. Children are very welcome indeed.
➕ 199 E2 ✉ Praia dos 3 Irmãos
☎ 282 459 688; www.facebook.com/oluis.
restaurante 🕐 Tue–Sun 9am–10pm

O Navegador €–€€
A reliable eatery that serves all kinds of fish and seafood. The specialities include kebabs, grilled fish and typical local *cataplanas*. The surprisingly large restaurant also boasts a terrace. It's located on a particularly beautiful *Insider Tip* section of the Ria de Alvor that's not open to through traffic, meaning you can enjoy an extremely peaceful, uninterrupted stroll along the promenade after dinner.
➕ 199 E2
✉ Zona Ribeirinha
☎ 282 412 375; http://navegadoralvor.webs.com
🕐 Daily noon–3pm, 4–11pm, until midnight in summer

Taberna Zé Morgadinho €
This tavern in Alvor's popular restaurant zone is an undying classic that retains all the authentic Portuguese flair of the good old days. Fishermen used to come here to eat their fill at the end of the nineteenth century. Guests sit at simple tables. Sardines aplenty are thrown on the grill during the holiday season.
➕ 199 E2 ✉ Zona Ribeirinha
☎ 929 058 153 🕐 Daily noon–11pm

LAGOS

Cachoa €€
This restaurant in an idyllic countryside location a little way outside Lagos is popular thanks to its beautiful garden terrace and its creatively presented cuisine. Tasty starters include salads and goats' cheese on apple slices. Good choices for your main course include lamb steaks, stuffed pork fillets or a tasty fish dish. Even the desserts are delicious. Vegetarian options are also available.
➕ 199 D2 ✉ Sitio de Cachoa
☎ 282 782 822; http://cachoa.50megs.com
🕐 Tue–Sat 6:30pm–midnight

Don Sebastião €€
Typical Portuguese cuisine has been served on this beautiful terrace in the pedestrian zone

149

since the late 1970s – a good guarantee of quality if ever there was one! The wide range of dishes on offer also includes some vegetarian meals. People-watchers will love it here – it's the perfect place to observe folk passing by as you eat.

🔢 199 D2
✉ Rua 25 de Abril 20–22
☎ 282 780 480; www.restaurantedon sebastiao.com 🕐 noon–10:30pm

Dos Artistas €€€

If you want to treat yourself, this classy restaurant with stylish décor and a beautiful terrace is the perfect place to be. The chefs are true artists who serve visually original dishes. They also offer four- to six-course set menus with suitable wines. It's great for vegetarians. You'll also have a fantastic time if you're a carnivore or enjoy eating lobster, mussels and other seafood. It's worth reserving a spot in advance.

🔢 199 D2 ✉ Rua Cândido dos Reis 68
☎ 282 760 659; www.artistasrestaurant.com
🕐 Mon–Sat 11am–2pm, 6pm–midnight

Fortaleza da Luz €–€€

If you're feeling peckish, head into the grounds of the old fortress (17th century) right next to the church in this holiday resort. You'll be able to dine in style there, unless it's been booked out for a wedding reception or a birthday bash. The menu is exceptionally good value for money. The terraces out in the garden are another highlight. You can sometimes enjoy live music while you eat.

🔢 199 D2 ✉ Avenida dos Pescadores 3
☎ 282 789 926; www.fortalezadaluz.com
🕐 11am–11pm

PORTIMÃO

Dona Barca €–€€

A traditional, authentic local eatery. It's a good place for fresh fish (the best is served from the grill). You'll find it tucked away by the old Arade bridge. Some of the seats are under the bridge itself. If you get lost, head towards the old brick chimney. **Insider Tip**

🔢 200 A3 ✉ Largo da Barca
☎ 282 484 189 🕐 Daily 6pm–midnight

Marisqueira Carvi €€€

A seafood restaurant that's a real hit with the locals. The friendly waiters will help you choose and present you with the day's fresh fish and seafood. Rice stews and curry dishes are also on offer. To cap it all, they always know the perfect wine to serve. An absolute pleasure!

🔢 200 A3 ✉ R. Direita 34 ☎ 282 417 912
🕐 noon–midnight, daily (except Tue)

O Mané €–€€

This typical, rustic *cervejaria* (brewery) is popular with the local population. For an authentic experience, try the *porco* (pork) cooked in a classic Alentejo style. The small grilled sardines with beans and rice (*carapauzinhos fritos*) taste wonderful. The fish selection is also delicious.

🔢 200 A3
✉ Rua Damião Luís Faria de Castro 1
☎ 282 423 496 🕐 6pm–midnight

SERRA DE MONCHIQUE

🛏 Jardim das Oliveiras €€

A beautiful, extremely rustic mountain restaurant in the Serra de Monchique. You'll spot the route to it (approx. 400m/440yds in length) on the right as you drive up the road from Monchique to Fóia. It's clearly signposted. They serve real home cooking – ham, sausages, game specialities (especially *javali* – wild boar), and dishes from the wood-fired oven. It's family friendly, too – kids can play out in the surrounding olive groves. **Insider Tip**

🔢 199 E5 ✉ Sítio do Porto Escuro
☎ 282 912 874; www.jardimdasoliveiras.com
🕐 Daily noon–10pm

Restaurante 1692 €€

An exemplary restaurant in the spa town of Caldas de Monchique. The terrace on the central, elm-lined square is particularly attractive during the warmer months of the year. Find a shady spot to sit down and enjoy the good Portuguese cuisine. If it starts to rain, gets too cool or all the seats are taken, find yourself a place inside instead. The restaurant also offers a good selection of wines.

🞦 199 E4
✉ In the centre of Caldas de Monchique
☎ 282 910 910; www.monchiquetermas.com
🕓 Daily 12:30–3pm, 7pm–10pm

Where to...
Shop

You'll find lots of great places for some retail therapy tucked away in the maze of streets in Lagos' Old Town. There are also lots of shops in Carvoeiro, but the gifts they sell tend to be mass-produced goods for the tourist market. It's more stylish in Monchique, where individual boutiques sell ceramics, *medronho* brandy and honey *(mel)*. Porches advertises itself as a traditional destination for pottery, although the selection there is limited to the big stores on the N125. They sell a good range of ceramics.

CULINARY TREATS

Start your shopping trip on the Praça Gil Eanes in **Lagos**. Don't miss the **market hall** in the Avenida dos Descobrimentos. You can buy fruit, vegetables, honey, spices, hot piri piri sauce, etc. in the upper section. If you'd prefer some good value wines, keep driving. Head a short way west of **Porches** and you'll come across **Insider Tip**

the headquarters of the Adega Cooperativa do Algarve **wine cooperative** (➤ 27, closed Mondays) on the N125 in Lagoa. They sell red, white and rosé wines. The sweet muscat dessert wine *(moscatel)* is of a higher quality (and costs more as a result). You can also buy wines direct from the growers at the **Quinta dos Vales vineyard** (➤ 29, Sítio dos Vales, Estômbar; www. quintadosvales.eu).

SHOPPING MALL

AlgarveShopping (www.algarve shopping.pt), a huge shopping complex on the N125 near Guia, is visited by large numbers of locals and tourists. The shops sell clothes, footwear, watches, accessories, and a great deal more besides.

MARKETS & FLEA MARKETS

The region's colourful flea and junk markets *(feiras de velharias)* are extremely popular with both locals and tourists alike. They're usually held in the morning. With any luck you'll find an original souvenir from the dealers, stall holders and local craftspeople who gather there. Ask at the nearest tourist office to find out about current dates. Most of the markets take place at regular intervals: on the 2nd Sunday of the month in **Ferragudo** (Zona Ribeirinha); on the 4th Sunday in **Lagoa** (Recinto da Fatacil); on the 1st Sunday in **Lagos** (Parque de Estacionamento do Complexo Desportivo); and on the 1st and 3rd Sunday of the month in **Portimão** (Parque de Feiras e Exposições). More con-ventional markets *(mercados)* are also held on fixed dates: on the 2nd Sunday of the month in **Lagoa** (the site opposite Fatacil); on the 1st Saturday in **Lagos** (by the Estádio Municipal); on the 4th Monday in **Odiáxere** (Largo do Moinho); and on the 2nd Friday of the month in **Monchique** (Largo do Mercado).

Where to...
Go Out

Praia da Rocha and Lagos are the most reliable destinations for a night or an evening out in the western Algarve. Carvoeiro also shows some signs of life after dark.

Stevie Ray's bar in Lagos (Rua Senhora da Graça, http://stevie-rays.com) is well-known for its live music, and you'll spot other places to go out at night in the surrounding Old Town district. The Auditório Municipal in Lagos' Parque das Freiras (Parque Dr. Júdice Cabral) is used as a venue for **open-air events**.

You'll find a **cinema** at the AlgarveShopping mall near Guia. If you fancy a change of scene, check out the ambitious **art exhibitions** organised by the Arte Algarve art association (www.artealgarve.net). Sometimes planned to coincide with colourful **summer events**, they're held in the big building of the Lagoa wine cooperative (on the N125). You'll see other exhibitions from Arte Algarve at the gallery in Ferragudo (Rua 25 de Abril 55–57).

LEISURE ACTIVITIES

Insider Tip Families with kids will love 🐟 **whale watching trips** and **boat tours** to the caves at the Ponta da Piedade. They set sail from Lagos. Boat trips along the picturesque rocky coast also set sail from Carvoeiro.

Other popular day trip destinations include: the 🐟 **Parque**

Zoológico de Lagos (➤ 135), about 10km (6mi) northwest of Lagos; the **Parque da Mina** (➤ 136), that lies inland between Portimão and Caldas de Monchique; and the spectacular **Fiesa Sand Sculpture Festival** (➤ 139) near Pêra (held between March and October). *Insider Tip* Visits to the **aqua parks** and **Zoomarine** (➤ 140) cost a pretty penny; they're only open in the warmer months. Sporty types can try wind surfing, kite surfing and standup paddleboarding with **Windsurf Point** (www.windsurfpoint.com) on the Meia Praia near Lagos and on the Praia do Martinhal by Sagres. The Praia do Beliche is a surfing beach near the Cabo de São Vicente. If you fancy **diving**, take the plunge at Sagres with such operators as **Divers Cape** (tel. 282 624 370; www.diverscape.com). Head east of Armação de Pêra towards Albufeira and you'll spot a signposted junction to the Quinta da Saudade **equestrian centre** (Vale Parra, tel. 964 942 929; www.cavalosquintadasaudade.com) where you can go **riding**. You can **hike** along the Via Algarviana and the Rota Vicentina long-distance routes. A beautiful section of trail, part of which runs along the cliffs, goes from Vila do Bispo to the **Cabo de São Vicente** (➤ 127). **Golf courses** include Vale de Milho Golf (http://valedemilho golf.com) and Vale da Pinta Golf (www.pestanagolf.com).

INFORMATION ON CULTURAL AND SPORTING EVENTS

You'll find the "Algarve Guia/Guide" available free of charge from tourist information offices throughout the region. This small but handy monthly publication will tell you everything you need to now about the festivals, events, exhibitions, sports fixtures and concerts that are taking place while you're on holiday.

Costa Vicentina

 **Little Treats**

Walking by the Waves

If you're feeling active, head down to the
Praia da Bordeira (➤ 163) and get your heart
pumping with a brisk walk along the sand.

Wonderful Views

Take in the scent of the sea breeze on the
Ponta da Arrifana (➤ 162). The views out over
the cliffs are breath-taking.

Riding through the Surf

If you love water sports and the Atlantic,
book a **surf course** (➤ 158)! They're available
for riders of all abilities.

Getting Your Bearings

If you're looking for mass tourism and giant hotels, then you've come to the wrong place! The Costa Vicentina is a region of rugged natural surroundings. Nature fans will love the wild scenery and surfers will love the waves. Travel here to escape the holiday hotspots and get to know a completely different side of the Algarve.

The region's cliffs and unsheltered beaches combine to form the wildly romantic scenery that dominates the Costa Vicentina. This section of coast begins north of the **Cabo de São Vicente**. Its highlights include such beaches as the **Praia do Amado**, the **Praia da Bordeira** and the **Praia de Monte Clérigo**. The difference between high and low tide is immense. What's more, the waves and currents can be dangerous, so never swim too far out to sea! Local barnacle collectors know the area like the backs of their hands. They risk their lives venturing out onto the razor-sharp cliffs to harvest goose barnacles *(percebes)*, a local delicacy.

The Atlantic is rougher and cooler on the Costa Vicentina than elsewhere in the Algarve. It's also home to more than half of Portugal's species of algae. The majority of these microorganisms float along the country's entire western flank and form the bottom of a food chain that keeps the wealth of fish and birds here alive. Ospreys, herons and storks have plenty to eat. If you're organising your own holiday, you'll find a good base in **Carrapateira**, **Aljezur** or

The beaches of the Costa Vicentina are a paradise for surfers and hikers alike

Praia de Monte Clérigo ㊺ Amoreira
Rogil
Carrascalinho
Monte Clérigo
Aljezur ㊹
Praia de Arrifana ㊻ Arrifana Vales
Ribeira de Alfambres

Parque Natural do Sudoeste Alentejano e Costa Vicentina

Monte Novo Chabouco
Monte Ruivo
Praia da Bordeira ㊼
Bordeira
㊽ **Carrapateira**
0 ___ 5 km
0 ___ 3 mi
Praia do Amado ⭐
Vilarinha
Pedralva
Pêro Queimado
Praia do Castelejo ㊾
Raposeira
Vila do Bispo

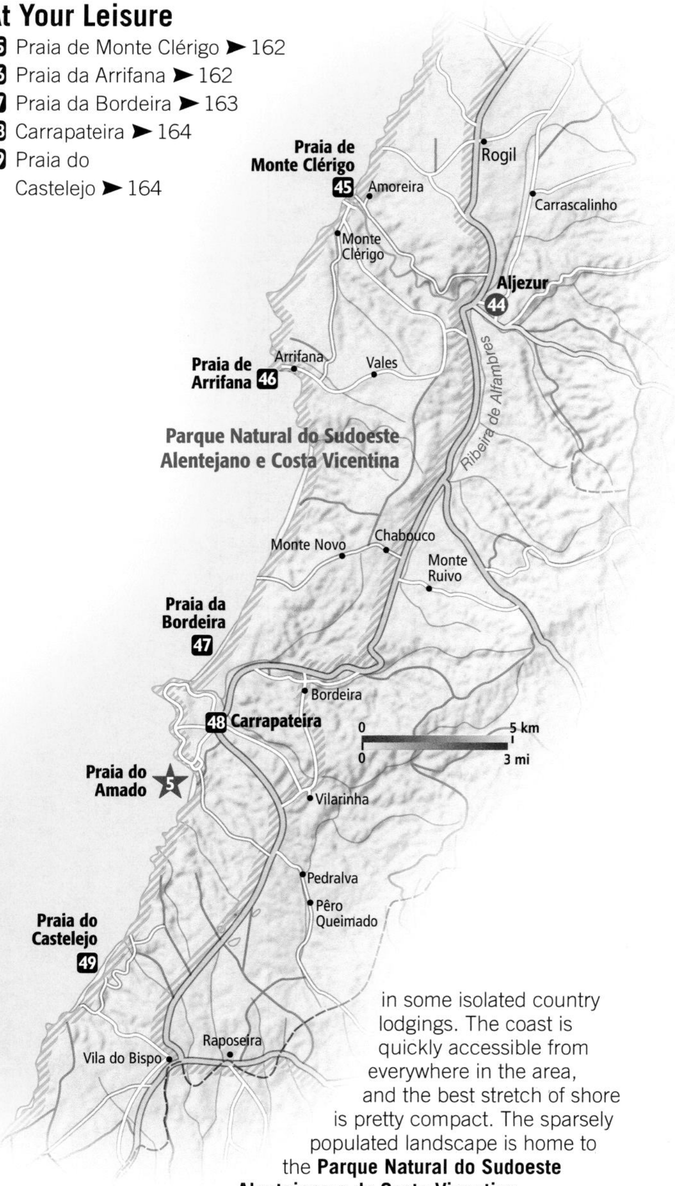

in some isolated country lodgings. The coast is quickly accessible from everywhere in the area, and the best stretch of shore is pretty compact. The sparsely populated landscape is home to the **Parque Natural do Sudoeste Alentejano e da Costa Vicentina**.

Perfect Days in...

The Perfect Day

With its rugged beaches and rocky coasts, the Costa Vicentina is first and foremost a place of natural beauty. To mix things up a bit, we've also added some little cultural destinations like Aljezur's ruined castle and its Municipal Museum into our itinerary. Round off your day by taking in the wonderful views at the Arrifana headland. You'll need a (rental) car for the trip.

Morning

Start your day by driving to one of the very best beaches on the Costa Vicentina, the ★**Praia do Amado** (➤ 158). It's usually filled with surfers gliding over the waves. If you don't want to have a go yourself, spend some time filling your camera's memory card with pictures of the panoramic view before heading down onto the beach from the large car park. If you'd like to take a stroll along the beach, spread a towel out on the sand or take a cooling dip in the Atlantic, you'd be better heading further north to the **47 Praia da Bordeira** (➤ 163) that lies on the mouth of a small river. The route there leads via the village of **48 Carrapateira** (➤ 164). Afterwards, drive to **44 Aljezur** for a spot of lunch. It's the most important inland town for miles around.

Afternoon

After lunch in **44 Aljezur** (➤ 160), drive or walk to the town's **ruined castle**. The site is open for anyone to visit at any time and guarantees a good view of the surrounding landscape. You can also pay a visit to Aljezur's small

Museu Municipal (Municipal Museum) when you make your way back to the lower part of town from the castle. The museum is dedicated to local and folk history.

From now on, you'll spend the rest of the day in the Aljezur area. Continue your voyage of discovery by exploring some more local beaches. As you travel around you'll often spot succulent plants (image above) growing in the dry ground or on the rocks above the shore. They can store water in their leaves for a very long time. Drive from Aljezur to the **45 Praia de Monte Clérigo** (► 162, image left), which has been awarded the prized "Blue Flag" for water purity on numerous occasions. Its size means that it's also suitable for **👪** families with kids. The **46 Praia da Arrifana** (► 162), flanked by towering walls of rock, boasts some spectacular views. There's only a limited number of places to park here, so depending on the season, you might have no choice but to get there on foot.

Jump back in your car and drive further west to the **Ponta da Arrifana** (► 162), the Arrifana headland that rises up high above the coast. The narrow road ends here. The views of the Atlantic, the cliffs, and the remains of the **Fortaleza de Arrifana** – a small, historic fortress – are quite simply fantastic.

Praia de Monte Clérigo
45

Aljezur
44

46
Praia de
Arrifana

Praia da
Bordeira
47

48 Carrapateira

Praia do
Amado **5**

Praia do
Castelejo
49

Evening
The **Restaurante O Paulo** (closed on Mondays) near the Fortaleza de Arrifana is a good place to stop for an evening meal.

⑤ Praia do Amado

Centuries ago, the Costa Vicentina coastal region needed to be protected from pirates. The large car parks at the entrance to the Praia do Amado are a sign that another kind of invader is flooding the coast today. Nature fans come here in droves to enjoy this fantastic stretch of sand to the southwest of Carrapateira. The Praia do Amado isn't any ordinary beach – its strong breakers make it an absolute paradise for surfers and body boarders alike.

You should only swim here if you take the usual precautions. The sand is clean, shines brightly in the sun, and stretches out over a length of about 1km (0.6mi) between some huge mounds of rock that also rise up behind parts of the beach. The country inland from the shore is undeveloped and the infrastructure is poor, allowing the Praia do Amado to remain blissfully unspoilt as a result.

Getting in the mood to surf with a dry run on the beach: the Praia de Amado is good for beginners

A Surfer's Paradise
A number of surf schools that offer courses have their base here. On some days, you'll see scores of surfers dotted around in the Atlantic. The Praia do Amado is considered a very good place for beginners, as the waves break early and roll for a long time. Before you head out into the water, you'll do warm ups, stretches and dummy runs on dry land. If you're feeling active but don't want to get your feet wet, take a brisk walk along the beach.

The **surf schools** on the Praia do Amado are mainly open during the warmer months of the year. The institutions here include the Future Surfing School (tel. 918 755 823; www.future-surf.com) and the Algarve Surf School (tel. 962 846 771; www.algarvesurfcamp.com). Make sure the course you're taking is held in English and check that all the equipment you need (board, neoprene wetsuit) is included in the price. Lessons are usually carried out in small groups. You can either arrange to meet your instructor

Right: You'll get some great views if you take a seat at one of the beach cafés

right on the Praia do Amado itself or be collected by one of their pick-up services elsewhere.

You'll need to shell out around €50–€60 per person to attend a **day course** (with lessons taught as part of a group). A seven-day surf camp at the Algarve Surf School costs around €345–€475 per person. The price includes surfing lessons, equipment and simple accommodation in communal rooms. **Week-long surf camps** are also offered by Fun Ride (tel. 967 607 480; www.funridesurfcamp.com) and Amado Surf Camp (tel. 927 831 568; www.amadosurf camp.com).

TAKING A BREAK

Seasonal refreshment stands with small terraces open up shop above the Praia do Amado (located between the car park and the entrance to the beach). They're a good place to take the weight off your feet, soak up the atmosphere and enjoy the beautiful views.

➕ 198 B3

INSIDER INFO

- You'll see strong **warnings of erosion damage** right behind the Praia do Amado – don't venture too far out onto the rocks.
- When your surf lessons are over for the day and most of the visitors have left, _Insider Tip_ kick back and enjoy the beautiful evening atmosphere.
- If you've got a robust car, you might like to drive along the track by the cliff-lined coast. It heads northwards from the Praia do Amado to the car park near the **Praia da Bordeira** (➤ 163). It then leads further on to the village of **Carrapateira** (➤ 164). The route is dusty and stony. It can be extremely irksome to get a flat tyre in this isolated area, so be careful! Stop by the side of the road from time to time and take a stroll down the small wooden walkways you'll find. They lead down to a type of viewing platform jutting out above the coast. If you don't want to drive, you can also take a walk along the track between the Praia do Amado and the Praia da Bordeira. Be warned, however – there's a chance you'll get pretty dusty if you meet a vehicle heading the other way!

44 Aljezur

Aljezur is the largest settlement for miles around, automatically making it an important regional hub. Home to 3,000 inhabitants, it lies in an agricultural landscape away from the coast. It's a relatively extensive place that's divided up into three parts – a lower town, an upper town, and a newer district from the 18th century that stands a short way away from the other two.

Following the heavy damages caused by the earthquake of 1755, the Algarve Bishopric pushed for the development of a new settlement that would slow down the exodus of people leaving the area. A new parish church, the Igreja Matriz, was raised from the rubble in the new part of town they chose to build. Aljezur itself sits on a shallow slope by a plain where two rivers, the **Ribeira das Alfambras** and the

Ribeira das Cercas, merge together to form the **Ribeira de Aljezur**. This small waterway heads northwest before pouring into the Atlantic by the Praia da Amoreira. In terms of its agriculture, the Aljezur district specialises in growing peanuts and starchy sweet potatoes.

Take a trip from Aljezur to the Praia de Monte Clérigo to watch the sun go down

The best place to visit is the upper part of town. It's dominated by the ruins of a **castelo** that can be seen from far and wide. According to a local source, this fortress is viewed as a symbol of the "struggles between the Christians and the Moors." This conflict harks back to the Middle Ages, when Aljezur lay in Moorish hands for many centuries.

INSIDER INFO

Insider Tip

- Sweet local specialities include sweet potato cake (*torta de batata-doce*) and sweet potato pudding (*pudim de batata-doce*).
- The N267, a relatively **quiet little road** to the east of Aljezur, leads into the Serra de Monchique (► 136) via Marmelete. Consider taking it – it's a good opportunity to breathe in some mountain air without having to drive along the much busier route that heads out to the hills from the north of Portimão.
- The N120 to the north of Aljezur runs inland to Odeceixe. You'll spot access roads leading to such **beaches** as the Praia da Amoreira (where the Ribeira de Aljezur meets the sea), the Praia da Carriagem and the Praia de Odeceixe at the mouth of the river Ceixe. Surfers and body boarders love the Praia de Odeceixe, where **there's often a good amount of wind.**

Even the town's name has Arabic origins, and was likely derived from the term *al jazira*. Meaning "the island", this moniker gives you an idea of how significant the river used to be to the settlement. At one point in time, Aljezur could even boast a river harbour. Unfortunately, the small waterway gradually silted up. The castle probably dates from the 10th century. It was brutally wrested from the Moors by Christian forces led by Paio Peres Correia – the Grandmaster of the Order of Santiago – in 1249. After the late Middle Ages, the castle began to fall into disrepair. You don't need a ticket to visit the ruins, as they're always open to visitors. It's worth driving or climbing up there for the view of the surrounding area alone. You can park right in front of the castle, although the drive up is pretty steep.

You'll also find the **Igreja da Misericórdia** (16th century) and the **Museu Municipal** – the Municipal Museum – in the upper part of town. The latter is housed in the former town hall and lets you dive a little deeper into the history of the area. The exhibits include pieces dating from the Neolithic, Roman and Moorish eras. There's also an informative folk history department with displays of such agricultural equipment as axes and hoes and a replica of a typical country kitchen.

Aljezur is a great base for exploring some **beaches**: the Praia da Arrifana (➤ 163) and the Praia de Monte Clérigo (➤ 162) are within easy reach. Tranquil Aljezur seems a world apart from Lagos (➤ 132) – the holiday centre of the western Algarve – yet it's only 30km (18mi) away.

TAKING A BREAK

Aljezur's market café near the river is popular with the locals. Don't worry if it's closed – you'll find some alternative options if you cross the small bridge over the water and head into the lower part of town.

A display case filled with Roman vases in the Museu Municipal

➕ 198 C5 🚌 Buses to Lagos and Odeceixe, etc.; www.eva-bus.com

Posto de Turismo
✉ Rua 25 de Abril 62
☎ 282 998 229;
www.cm-aljezur.pt

Museu Municipal de Aljezur
✉ Largo 5 de Outubro
🕐 Tue–Sat 9–1pm, 2–5pm
💶 €2 (Combiticket).
Tickets also valid for other museums. In the Rua do Castelo: the Casa-Museu Pintor José Cercas (the house of a local painter, 1914–1992) and the Museu de Arte Sacra. In the Rua de Santo António: the Museu Antoniano.

At Your Leisure

over the dunes to the pristine sandy beach. You'll spot a small group of weekend and holiday cottages climbing the rocky slope by the shore. It's often very quiet outside the summer season.
⊞ 198 C5

46 Praia da Arrifana
Sheltered at the back by some **steep coastal cliffs**, the Praia da Arrifana sits next to the wide Arrifana bay. A lot of the **sand** gets swallowed up at high tide. When driving down here, prepare to encounter some bends, steep slopes and limited parking space. Some people leave their vehicles at the top and head to the Praia da Arrifana on foot – though bear in mind that you'll have to walk back up again later on!

The beach isn't the only place worth visiting here – check out the nearby headland known as the **Ponta da Arrifana**. The road to this promontory ends near the re-

45 Praia de Monte Clérigo
This beautiful beach that's a hit with families can be reached by heading northwest of Aljezur (► 160). The last part of the route is signposted. A walkway leads

The road winds past houses and fish restaurants on its way to the Praia da Arrifana

The Costa Vicentina is a popular surfing destination

mains of the **Fortaleza de Arrifana**, a fortress dating from the 1600s.

Insider Tip The impressive views of the coast are more interesting than the ruins themselves. When the conditions are right, you'll see beautiful sweeping vistas filled with mighty flanks of rock, outcrops jutting into the water, stone ledges that look like shark fins, and a mighty sea that often surges and foams beneath your feet.

Arrifana bay is more sheltered and boasts a small fishing harbour. The freestanding, needle-like rock there is called the Pedra de Agulha. You'll see the Praia da Arrifana in the distance.

✚ 198 B4

⑰ Praia da Bordeira

The names of this beach and the river estuary nearby can cause some confusion. The Praia da Bordeira, which lies very close to the village of Carrapateira, is also known as the Praia da Carrapateira. The **small river** is called both the Ribeira da Carrapateira and the Ribeira da Bordeira, depending on which map you use and who you talk to. This waterway doesn't always reach the Atlantic. At these times, it feeds a kind of **lagoon** and peters out before it arrives at the sea. It's often possible to ford the river when the water level's at the right height. You can also reach the beach via the stairs from a car park higher up.

If you're travelling from Carrapateira, you can get to this car park by keeping the sea in your sights and driving down a stretch of track that goes upwards and left towards the Praia do Amado (▶ 86). When you reach a fork in the road, turn right. The relatively long wooden staircase offers wonderful views of the broad beach. It may be in poor condition towards the bottom. The Praia da Bordeira is extremely wide and

Costa Vicentina

A windmill in Carrapateira

about 3km (2mi) long. It's rough, isolated, unsheltered and doesn't offer any shade. It's often also buffeted by the wind and there are no tourist facilities in sight. This makes it an absolute dream for nature fans! Rust-brown cliffs rise up along part of the Praia da Bordeira, and it's flanked by dunes at the back.

⊞ 198 B3

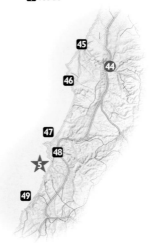

48 Carrapateira

This slightly larger village lies inland from the coast. It's mainly seen as a strategic base for travellers who use it as a starting point for trips to such attractive beaches as the Praia do Amado (▶ 158) and the Praia da Bordeira (▶ 163). It has some simple accommodation. Eye-catching local sights include the old windmill on the hill and the inland dunes. The exhibits at the **Museu do Mar e de Terra** deal with life in the countryside and at sea.

The layout of the village seems quite disorganised – some of the houses are separated by astonishingly large green spaces and clusters of agaves. There are a few eateries on the main street. All the life seems to get sucked out of Carrapateira outside the holiday season. You'll find a couple of quiet beaches between Carrapateira and Aljezur: the Praia Vale Figueiras and the Praia do Canal.

⊞ 198 B3

Museu do Mar e de Terra
✉ Rua do Pescador ☎ 282 970 000
🕐 Tue–Sat 10am–1pm and 1:30pm–4:30pm
💰 €3

49 Praia do Castelejo

This long, raw, somewhat narrower beach in the Vila do Bispo municipality stands in an unsheltered spot by the Atlantic. The waves here can be turbulent. The cliffs behind the sand are sometimes used as a launching site for paragliders. The beach is also popular with surfers. The Praia do Castelejo forms part of a trio of dreamy beaches along with the Praia da Cordoama and the Praia da Barriga nearby. A number of umbrella pines add some greenery to the landscape further inland.

⊞ 198 A2

Right: The Praia da Cordoama – a paradise for surfers and nature fans alike

Where to...
Stay

Prices
for a double room per night in the high season
€ under 90 euros   €€ 90–150 euros   €€€ over 150 euros

ALJEZUR

Amazigh Hostel €

Travellers from all over the world come to stay at this nice hostel. The room prices are low, and the rates for dormitory beds are even lower. It's pleasantly furnished and the staff are friendly. As well as rooms in the hostel itself, they also rent out whole villas in the surrounding area. These fall into a whole other category when it comes to price and quality (€€–€€€), but they can be worth a look if you're in a larger group.

🚩 198 C4
✉ Rua da Ladeira 5
☎ 282 997 502; www.amazighostel.com

Herdade Monte do Sol €€–€€€

The accommodation at this rural establishment on a country estate outside Aljezur consists of several small houses that all come complete with a terrace and a small kitchen. Spacious grounds surround the pool. A tip for getting here: whatever you do, make sure to print off the English route description from their homepage before you arrive.

🚩 198 C5 ✉ Herdade Monte do Sol ☎ 282 997 358; www.herdademontedosol.com

CARRAPATEIRA

Pensão das Dunas €

A traditional, family-run guest house with a friendly atmosphere. You can choose between six holiday apartments and four rooms. Each of the holiday apartments comes equipped with a kitchen. All of the accommodation is offered at a very reasonable price. Surfers like using the guest house as a base for their marine adventures in the area.

🚩 198 B3
✉ Rua da Padaria 9
☎ 282 973 118; www.pensao-das-dunas.pt

PEDRALVA

Aldeia da Pedralva €€–€€€

New life has been breathed into Pedralva – a village situated away from the coast – thanks to private investment, extensive restoration and a shrewd plan to cater to the alternative tourism market. As hoped, demand has been brisk. The extended village is now home to more than two dozen houses of different sizes and facilities that are rented out to guests via a central reservations office. The village is a great place to enjoy the peace and quiet of the countryside (➤ 40). You'll automatically feel yourself sinking into a slower pace of life while you're here. It's an extremely relaxing experience! The nearest beaches are an accessible distance away – it takes around 10–15 minutes to get there by car. The Aldeia da Pedralva also has a pool.

🚩 198 B3
✉ Take the signposted junction to Aldeia da Pedralva on the country highway between Vila do Bispo and Carrapateira, Rua de Baixo–Casa da Pedralva
☎ 282 639 342; www.aldeiadapedralva.com

REGUENGO

🏠 Reguengo €

The sun produces the energy and a spring provides the water at this alternative hinterland retreat. Guests can choose to stay in rooms or apartments. The soft colours on the walls add to the comfortable ambience, which is enhanced by the yoga and meditation sessions on offer. Run by Palmira and Stephan Biesenbach, Reguengo is anything but mainstream. It's also well suited to families with kids, thanks not in small part to the childcare they organise during the holiday season. To get here, drive to the southeast of Odeceixe via Zambujeira de Baixo. It can be tricky to find, so download the PDF of directions from the website before you arrive. The rates lie at the upper end of its price category.

Insider Tip

➕ 199 D5 ✉ Reguengo, detailed directions are available to download from the website
☎ 282 911 901; www.reguengo.de

Where to...
Eat and Drink

Prices
for a three-course set menu without drinks or service
€ under 20 euros   €€ 20–35 euros   €€€ over 35 euros

ALJEZUR

Pont'a Pé €–€€

This bar-restaurant in the lower part of Aljezur is popular with the locals. You'll find it near the footbridge over the small river. The menu includes salads and omelettes as well as more elaborate dishes like a fish *cataplana* for two people. For dessert, try the delicious specialities made from sweet potatoes *(batata-doce)*. The terrace fills up fast.

➕ 198 C5
✉ Largo da Liberdade 12
☎ 282 998 104; www.pontape.pt
🕐 Mon–Sat 9am–11pm

CARRAPATEIRA

L-Colesterol €

This simple, no-frills restaurant with ecological leanings and a humorous name serves up a variety of fish dishes and fresh vegetables harvested from the garden. If you like, you can also stay the night in a room at the L-Colesterol Bed & Breakfast.

➕ 198 B3
✉ Horta do Rio
☎ 282 998 147; http://l-colesterol.com
🕐 Daily 10am–9pm

PEDRALVA

Sítio da Pedralva €€

This tasteful main restaurant sits in the old village of Aldeia da Pedralva (► 41) that's been beautifully restored. The specialities include house-style dried cod and lamb ribs with sweet potato purée. You can have a stroll through the village after dinner.

➕ 198 B3
✉ Take the junction to Aldeia da Pedralva from the country highway between Vila do Bispo and Carrapateira
☎ 282 639 342; www.aldeiadapedralva.com
🕐 Daily noon–3pm and 7pm–11pm

Costa Vicentina

O Paulo €€

Housed in a low, single-storey building with lots of windows, this cosy restaurant sits in a wind-whipped spot on the Ponta da Arrifana. It's close to the remains of the headland's fortress, the Fortaleza de Arrifana. Fish and shellfish are the mainstays of the menu. They're tasty, well cooked, and nicely presented. *Insider Tip* You can't leave without taking a short after-dinner walk to the magnificent viewpoint nearby.

🔷 198 B4 ✉ Arrifana, near the Fortaleza
☎ 282 995 184; www.restauranteopaulo.com
🕙 Tue–Sun noon–3pm, 7pm–10:30pm

PRAIA DA ARRIFANA

Restaurante da Praia €€

It's not just your taste buds that are in for a treat at this beach restaurant above the Praia da Arrifana – you can also feast your eyes on the views outside! The menu is stuffed with fresh fish and salads (some with seafood). If you come on the right day, you can also try goose barnacles *(percebes)*, a local delicacy.

🔷 198 B4 ✉ above the beach ☎ 282 998 527; http://restaurantepraiaarrifana.com
🕙 June–mid-Sept, daily 9:30am–midnight; rest of the year 10:30am–8pm

Where to... Shop

The Costa Vicentina is a region of natural beauty, not a shopping paradise. You can shop and get hiking supplies at the markets, however.

The flea market in **Aljezur** is held every 1st Sunday in the month from around 9am–1pm at the Escola Primária dos Vales. A market also takes place by the Junta de Freguesia building every 4th Sunday in the month. Aljezur's *Feira da Terra* – a festival dedicated *Insider Tip* to egionally grown products – is held every Saturday in July and August. You can get essentials from the tiny market hall near the river at other times.

Where to... Go Out

You won't find much nightlife on the Costa Vicentina. If you fancy a drink, head to Aljezur, to the small square on the road through Carrapateira, or to the seasonal surfer hangouts above the Praia do Amado. The area is more geared to sporty types and nature fans who love the outdoors, although it does get lively during the folk festivals.

FOLK FESTIVALS

Folk festivals breathe some life into this peaceful region. This is particularly true in August, when **Carrapateira** and **Odeceixe** celebrate festivities on varying dates. It's also worth seeing the *Festa dos Pescadores* ("Festival of Fishermen") at the small harbour in Arrifana bay (last weekend in July), and *Noite A*, a multicultural party in **Aljezur** (late August). A traditional *feira* ("**fair**") is held in **Odeceixe** at the start of September and in **Aljezur** at the end of the same month. The *Festival da Batata-doce* also takes place in Aljezur at the beginning of the milder winter season (the last weekend in November or the first weekend in December). This event revolves around the sweet potatoes grown in the region.

Walks & Tours

1 FARO'S OLD TOWN

Walk

DISTANCE: 1.8km (1.1 miles)
TIME: 45–60 minutes
START/FINISH: Jardim Manuel Bivar ✚ 202 C2/3

Faro's cosy Old Town begins behind the Arco da Vila

Faro's historic quarter is full of surprises. Let yourself drift through the streets that originated in the Middle Ages. Whitewashed houses act as a reminder of the city's Moorish heritage. The cathedral is worth a visit. Part of the route you'll take follows the mighty city wall. If you come at the right time, the Old Town will be filled with an unusual sound – the clatter of storks' beaks.

❶–❷

Start off at the **Jardim Manuel Bivar**, the small green area behind the picturesque marina. It's located within the walls of the Old Town. Head towards the tourist information office in the Rua da Misericórdia where you can pick up a city map and get some more information. Afterwards, walk into the historic district through the **Arco da Vila** next door, a gate in the city wall that was restored in the 19th century.

❷–❸

Once you're through the Arco da Vila, go straight on and walk up the slight incline along the **Rua do Município**. Don't forget to turn round and admire the view. The gate looks particularly photogenic from this perspective! If they haven't flown away, you'll sometimes see a pair of storks on the top.

8–4

The Rua do Município bends to the right and leads to part of the **Largo da Sé**, the square in front of Faro's cathedral. You'll be greeted by orange trees and the solid structure of the **cathedral** (► 100) itself as you arrive. The building's origins date from 13th/14th century.

Orange trees line the large square in front of Faro's cathedral

Jardim Manuel Bivar

Arco da Vila
Rua da Misericórdia

R. do Albergue

R. Rasquinho

R. do Município

R. José M. Bandeiro

Centro Ciência Viva do Algarve

Largo da Sé

Restaurante Cidade Velha

Arco do Repouso

R. de Domingos Guieiro

Sé

R. do Repouso

Praça do Afonso III.

Muralha

Museu Municipal

R. da Porta

Rua do Trem

Rua Comandante Francisco Manuel

Largo do Castelo

Largo de São Francisco

Rua Nova do Castelo

0   50 m
0   50 yd

Walks & Tours

Insider Tip

You'll get the best views (and the best photos!) if you head a little further round the cathedral to the right (to the side with the entrance). Plan at least half an hour extra if you'd like to see inside the cathedral and climb all the way up the tower.

4–5
Head back to where the Rua do Município joins the square. Turn so that the cathedral is behind you on your right hand side and walk round the back of the building. After this manoeuvre, you should automatically find yourself in the **Rua de Domingos Guieiro**.

5–6
Walk a short way along the Rua de Domingos Guieiro until you reach the next square, the **Praça do Afonso III**. The square is home to a prominent monument of its namesake, King Afonso III (1210–1279). The monarch is given pride of place in the square because Faro was wrested back from Moorish hands during his reign. The entrance to the **Museu Municipal** (➤ 101), Faro's municipal museum, is also located in the square. It's housed in the former convent of Nossa Senhora da Assunção. Add another hour to your tour if you want to visit the museum, which contains a particularly beautiful, well-preserved cloister.

6–7
It's time to leave the elongated Praça do Afonso III. Turn your back to the museum's entrance. Veer right and walk along the **Rua do Repouso**, the next peaceful street.

7–8
Stroll a short way along the Rua do Repouso and you'll reach the **Arco do Repouso**, another historic city gate.

8–9
Walk through the Arco do Repouso and leave the historic quarter. Look to your right on the other side of the gate to see a picture made of blue-and-white tiles. It depicts a historical scene from 1269: *Outorga do Foral aos Mouros forros por D. Afonso III* ("King Alfonso III granting rights to the defeated Moors"). Walk for about 300m along the outside of the impressive **city walls**. If you can see the large car parks on the Largo de São Francisco on your left, you're in the right place.

9–10
At the end of the wall, keep walking straight on until you reach a route to the right that runs parallel to the water. It's called the **Rua Comandante Francisco Manuel** and is closed to traffic.

10–11
As you stroll along the Rua Comandante Francisco Manuel, you'll be flanked by the restored city walls to your right and an old set of train tracks on a narrow embankment to your left. Few trains use this route, so it won't spoil the view. Graffiti artists like to get creative on the walls here from time to time. This **stretch of the promenade** is very pleasant indeed. It leads past the 🚸 **Centro Ciência Viva do Algarve** (www.ccvalg.pt), a small, interactive science centre that's geared to children and younger teens. As you reach the end of the street you'll see your starting point – the **Jardim Manuel Bivar** – coming into view. Sit down here for a rest and admire the harbour.

2 TO THE CABO DE SÃO VICENTE

Walk

DISTANCE: 13km (8 miles)
TIME: 4–5 hours   **START:** Vila do Bispo ✚ 198 B2
FINISH: Cabo de São Vicente ✚ 198 A1

A wonderful end to your hike: a fresh breeze and magnificent views of an untamed sea

This half-day hike will take you to the Cabo de São Vicente, a dreamy corner of Portugal that's whipped by the wind and waves. The route to the southwest of Vila do Bispo runs through some beautiful, isolated landscapes high above the Atlantic. You'll need to plan ahead. Get in touch with a taxi company well in advance (Taxi T are considered reliable: tel. 964 858 517; www.taxi-t.com) and ask them to pick you up from the Cabo de São Vicente after your walk. Depending on your fitness level and how much time you have, you could also walk back along the same 13km (8mi) route. Alternatively, park a second car near the Cape.

❶–❷
The hike starts on the outskirts of **Vila do Bispo** at the *Mercado Municipal*, the market building. You can stock up on fruit there (except Sun) or take a break in the small cafeteria. Follow the red and white markings of the GR11, a trail which coincides with the "Historical Route" of the Rota Vicentina at this point. You'll see it from the market in Vila do Bispo. The route initially runs along a quiet side road and leads up a slight incline past houses and fields where such crops as broad beans, tomatoes and peppers are grown depending on the season. Turn around and enjoy the view

Walks & Tours

back to Vila do Bispo. If you spot a dirt track joining the path on your right after **2.1km (1.3mi)**, you're going the right way.

🎇–🎇

A eucalyptus grove to the right dates from the time of the Salazar dictatorship. These trees were introduced in the 60s/70s to make a quick profit for the paper industry. Beautiful meadows and pastures accompany the trail as you continue on your way. The route then leads along a wide, navigable dirt track that's bordered by fences. It's flat here, and you'll spy the sea in the distance on the right before it temporarily disappears from view. **4km (2.5mi)** on from Vila do Bispo you'll see a GR11 sign pointing to the Cabo de São Vicente. It says it's 10km (6mi) away, but you can ignore 1km (0.6mi) of that as you'll take a shorter, more beautiful alternative route later on.

🎇–🎇

The hike continues along a broad path that leads through a wonderful, secluded lowland landscape. You'll spot a **control tower** for monitoring shipping off in the distance. Rockrose and low pines mingle in among the vegetation. The route isn't particularly difficult, but there's no shade to speak of to shelter you from the sun. At some point you'll spot an optional track that branches off to the **Ponta Ruiva**, a coastal lookout point.

TAKING A BREAK

There aren't any settlements along the route, so you won't find anywhere to stop for refreshments. Bring a picnic with you instead and eat it at an exposed spot high over the coast with a view of the sea. Alternatively, you'll usually find a couple of snack stands at the car park by the Cabo de São Vicente.

The main route continues a short distance inland.

🎇–🎇

You'll catch another glimpse of the ocean on the right. You'll also soon see the Cabo de São Vicente's lighthouse rising up in the distance. **6km (3.75mi)** on from Vila do Bispo you'll find a fork in the isolated path. Take care: don't follow the GR11 inland (it's marked by a signpost that says it's 8km to the Cabo de São Vicente). Instead, take the **Fishermen's Trail** on the Rota Vicentina that's lined with green and blue markings. A sign reads: Praia do Telheiro 3km, Cabo de São Vicente 7km. This is the right way to go.

🎇–🎇

Stumpy junipers grow all around, and the greenery merges with the blue of the sea to form a wonderful view to your right. The extremely low vegetation is caused by the wind that presses the plants into the ground. You won't see any villages or houses for a long way in either direction. Keep an eye open for the markings along the Rota Vicentina. They're painted on stones and special wooden stakes. At this point in the route, you can start using the lighthouse on the Cape as a landmark to guide you on. At first, the track is around 150m (490ft) from the cliffs. The further you go, however, the closer it gets to the edge. The path becomes narrower and stonier as it leads downwards past clusters of rockrose and juniper. The route gets particularly bumpy as it runs above the **Praia do Telheiro**, a beautiful bay. Be careful: don't let yourself be distracted by the spectacular scenery as you walk!

🎇–🎇

You're now just 4km (2.5mi) from the Cape. Feel the wind in your face and the salt on your skin.

The views are spectacular. The path is shaded by junipers and partially covered in sand. You'll also spot a dwarf palm tree here and there. Once again, pay attention to the markings along the trail! At some point you'll see a sign reminding you to respect your natural surroundings – please do what it says and stick to the path. The route leads down into a small gully. Later, as you reach the edge of the cliffs, the terrain becomes extremely stony. Place your feet very carefully here – it's not a good idea to take photos while you walk. The last stretch of track to the Cape follows the GR11 (recognisable from its white and red markings). It's impossible to get lost if you head towards the lighthouse. You'll be brought back to civilisation rather abruptly when you reach the paved road that leads up to the Cabo de São Vicente (► 127) – the thoroughfare greets you with engine noise and car parks. The views from the Cape here are even better than anything you've seen so far.

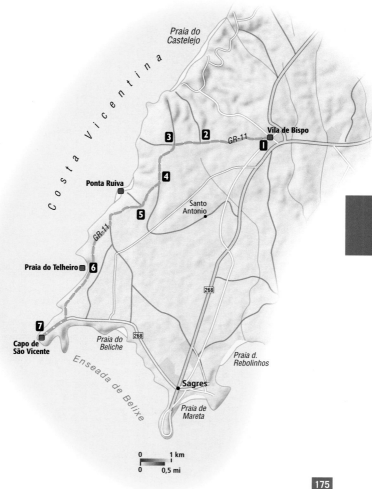

3 THE SERRA DE MONCHIQUE
Driving Tour

LENGTH: 84km (52 miles)
TIME: 1 day **START/FINISH:** Portimão
✛ 200 A3

It's time to head into the mountains!
Unlike the Algarve's coast, the Serra
de Monchique is a landscape filled
with lush greenery. Its climate is
also different. This driving tour is a
great way to explore further inland
and visit Fóia, the loftiest point in
the region that stands at a proud
altitude of 902m (2,959ft). You'll
be able to see whether or not this
peak is shrouded in cloud before
you leave the coast. If it is, plan
to make the trip another day – the
beautiful views from up here are a
vital part of the experience.

❶–❷
It's not hard to navigate here from
the outskirts of **Portimão**. Just
head northwards inland towards
the mountains of the Serra de
Monchique – they're easy enough
to spot! Take the N124, then the
N266. The region becomes greener
as you drive. The foothills are also

home to white storks. Instead of
staying on the main road, take the
right turn to Alferce shortly before
you reach the entrance to **Rasmalho**.
Keep your eyes peeled – the sign
to it isn't exactly obvious.

❷–❸
The small side road you're now
driving along follows a winding
route through the verdant, secluded
landscape. You'll see a little valley
filled with oranges and the odd
olive tree, cork oak and country
house dotted about here and there.
You've already reached the foothills
of the Serra de Monchique, a lush
world filled with many shades of
green. Drive carefully – it's not
uncommon for herds of cows to
trot across the street in front of you.
You'll see a crystal-clear river –
the Ribeira de Odelouca – on your
right-hand side. 9km (5.5mi) after
taking the turnoff by Rasmalho,

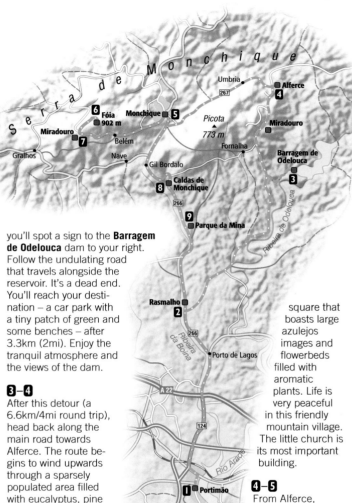

Umbria
267
Alferce
4

6 Fóia **Monchique** **5**
902 m
Miradouro
7
Belém
Picota
773 m
Miradouro

Grahos
Nave
Fornalha
Barragem de
Odelouca

• Gil Bordalo
3

8 **Caldas de**
Monchique
266

9
Parque da Mina

Ribeira de Odelouca

Rasmalho
2

Ribeira
da Boina
266

• Porto de Lagos

A 22

124

Rio Arade

1 **Portimão**

0   2 km
0   1 mi

you'll spot a sign to the **Barragem de Odelouca** dam to your right. Follow the undulating road that travels alongside the reservoir. It's a dead end. You'll reach your destination – a car park with a tiny patch of green and some benches – after 3.3km (2mi). Enjoy the tranquil atmosphere and the views of the dam.

3–**4**

After this detour (a 6.6km/4mi round trip), head back along the main road towards Alferce. The route begins to wind upwards through a sparsely populated area filled with eucalyptus, pine and cork oak trees. The elevated road to Alferce lets you catch glimpses of the Odelouca dam in the distance. Stop at a *miradouro* (viewpoint) and enjoy the view. The Picota massif rises up to a height of 774m (2,539ft) on your left. The cork oaks become more and more abundant as you drive. When you reach Alferce, you'll spot the Largo da Igreja de Alferce, a small village square that boasts large azulejos images and flowerbeds filled with aromatic plants. Life is very peaceful in this friendly mountain village. The little church is its most important building.

4–**5**

From Alferce, take the N267 in a southwesterly direction around the northern part of the Picota massif – a landscape filled with eucalyptus trees – to **Monchique** (➤ 136), the main mountain town where a number of white houses cover the hillside. Pay a visit to the Igreja Matriz church with its Manueline portal and its sculpture of Mary that you'll see over the altar.

Walks & Tours

The Serra's wilder mountain weather is used to generate wind energy

5–6

It's 8km (5mi) from Monchique to the 902m (1,260ft)-high **Fóia**. You'll pass a few roadside restaurants as you drive. The scent of eucalyptus fills the air above the winding route. Don't be put off by the antenna masts and the large parking lot you'll see up on the peak. As soon as you turn your back to them, you'll get magnificent, unobstructed views of the coast.

6–7

Follow the same route back down from Fóia. After around 2km (1.25mi) or so you'll see another *miradouro* (viewpoint) to the right. Leave your car at one of the car parks that's separated from the road. The views are just as beautiful here as up on the summit, and you won't be put off by any antennas nearby. There's also a spring where you can cool off with a splash of fresh mountain water.

7–8

After visiting the *miradouro*, drive onwards via Monchique and choose the direct route to the south along the N266 towards Portimão. It's 24km (15mi) from Monchique to

Portimão, but don't rush the journey in one fell swoop. On the first part of the route, take a detour to **Caldas de Monchique** (➤ 136), a small spa resort that sits in a valley away from the mountain road. Park on the outskirts of the village, take a stroll through its small centre and explore the park with its shady trees. You can also cool off at the refreshing mountain spring.

8–9

Follow the road as it heads down from Caldas de Monchique and out of the mountains. Families with kids will particularly enjoy making an extra stop at the ⛏️**Parque da Mina** (➤ 136). Otherwise, head back to Portimão.

TAKING A BREAK

The Bar O Tascoi in the tiny centre of **Caldas de Monchique**, a historic spa town, is an absolutely perfect place to stop for some drinks and snacks. If you'd like to eat something more sumptuous, head to **Restaurante 1692** (also in Caldas de Monchique). Find a lovely place to sit out on the large terrace.

4 ALONG THE ECOVIA
Cycling Tour

LENGTH: 42km (26 miles)
TIME: 1 Day
START/FINISH: Cabanas de Tavira ✚ 206 B1

This bike tour heads east from Cabanas de Tavira towards Vila Real de Santo António along the Ecovia (a.k.a. the Ecovia Litoral), a long-distance cycle track. A word of warning: large parts of the route run along the road. Portuguese cycle tracks aren't up to the same standard you might find elsewhere in Europe (e.g. in the Netherlands). Cabanas de Tavira, the start and end point of the tour, is a great place to set off: it's home to MegaSport (tel. 289 393 044 and 962 010 661; www.mega sport.pt), a company that runs a cycle hire station at the Pedras da Rainha

A stop for a rest and a photo along the route

hotel (➤ 82) from March to October/ November. Make sure your bike has a good lock. You'll spot the Ecovia thanks to the little posts with yellow markings by the side of the track. Keep your eyes peeled for these as you cycle! Try to remember the route on the trip out – you'll be coming back the same way later. Don't forget to bring lots of water and your swimming things!

1–2
After arriving in **Cabanas de Tavira** (➤ 68), cycle to the Avenida Ria Formosa, the promenade that runs

Walks & Tours

It's worth making a detour to Cacela Velha on the return leg

parallel to the canal. At the end of the promenade (where it bends to the left), keep cycling straight ahead along the dirt track. Then turn left and ride round the historic fortress of Fortaleza São João da Barra (not open to visitors). The surrounding landscape is filled with almond and fig trees. The route isn't marked out very well at first, but you'll soon see signposts pointing out the Ecovia as you cycle on. For a short while, the cycle route runs along the same path as the Camino de Santiago. You'll quickly come across orange plantations and carob trees.

A short stretch of the Ecovia runs along the busy N125 before heading off down a side road that leads past the Robinson Club and the turn-off to Cacela Velha. It's best to save the detour to this picturesque village for the return leg of your journey.

The next section of the road – lined with carob and almond trees – has lots of ups and downs to test your legs. It also draws close to the N125 for a time, before mercifully moving away from the highway once again. You'll eventually reach **Manta Rota**.

2–3

Cycle through Manta Rota. Your tour continues through the inland landscape. The small road you're on soon merges into a very nice stretch of combined footpath and cycle track. This leads through a meadowed area to **Altura**, the next town (around 1km/0.6mi away).

When you arrive there, you'll come out at the double-laned road running into town. Go right and cycle past the Eurotel, a boxy hotel.

3–4

After leaving Altura, the Ecovia runs along the busy N125 for around 1.5km (1mi). Unfortunately, there isn't a dedicated cycle path. It's an unpleasant stretch of route with no redeeming features.

Conceição

Cabanas de Tavira

125

Tavira

Turn right where you see a sign to Cabeço beach. Thankfully, the trail then runs along a beautiful side road through a pine forest.

Around 300m (330yds) before you reach the walkway to the **Praia do Cabeço**, the Ecovia leads left into the pine forest. Before you go that way, treat yourself to a detour to the Praia do Cabeço itself. It's important to lock your bikes up properly. Cool off with a quick dip in the refreshing waves.

4–5

You're in for a real treat after making the short detour to the Praia do Cabeço: the Ecovia now leads through a beautiful pine forest. You'll see a bird-watching hide on a **lake** to the left. The waters here are filled with reeds. A fence separates the lake from the footpath and cycle track. The route then travels out of the shady pine trees along a sunny stretch that leads into **Monte Gordo** (➤ 79), a holiday resort.

6–7

Explore Vila Real de Santo António. Whatever you do, don't miss the beautiful promenade that runs along the **Rio Guadiana** (on the Portuguese-Spanish border) or the Praça do Marquês de Pombal, the town's main square that boasts a church, an obelisk and a selection

Castro
Marim

São
Bartolomeu

Vila Real de
Santo António

A 22

Santa Rita
Morgadinha

Vila Nova
de Cacela

125

5 Monte Gordo

4

3 Altura

Praia do Cabeço

2 Manta Rota

0   2 km

0   1 mi

7

Cacela Velha

5–6

Monte Gordo and its apartments might be a little disappointing after the dreamy natural landscape you've just left behind. But never fear – the large stretches of beach here are immaculate. Cycle along the promenade and down the road between Yellow and Vasco da Gama, two boxy hotels.

As you're leaving Monte Gordo, you'll find the start of a proper bike path that runs parallel to the street. The Ecovia now travels though areas of pine trees belonging to the Mata Nacional das Dunas Litorais de Vila Real de Santo António **nature reserve** and heads straight to **Vila Real de Santo António** (➤ 76). The Ecovia ends in this small city, 214km (133mi) from where it started at the Cabo de São Vicente in the west.

of terrace cafés. Grab some refreshments before heading back along the same route via Monte Gordo, Altura and Manta Rota.

There's only one change on the way back: after you leave Manta Rota, make sure to make a short detour left to **Cacela Velha** (➤ 79), a tiny, picturesque village with spectacular views out over the eastern offshoots of the Parque Natural da Ria Formosa. The village church is the best vantage point. Afterwards, return to the main track and make your way back to where you started in **Cabanas de Tavira**.

Insider
Tip

TAKING A BREAK

It's worth taking a break at the Praça do Marquês de Pombal in **Vila Real de Santo António**. It boasts some large, inviting terraces, including the one at the Puro Café. An extra bonus: you can keep an eye on your bikes while you're there.

5 EXPLORING THE ALENTEJO
Tour

LENGTH: 490km (305 miles)
TIME: 4 days **START:** Vila Real de Santo António ✚ 206 C2
FINISH: Lagos ✚ 199 D2

Culture vultures should check out the Convento de Nossa Senhora da Conceição, the Clarissan convent in Beja

Come and explore the Alentejo, the sparsely populated region that neighbours the Algarve to the north. The first part of the route will show you the vast inland areas, while the second will show you the beauty of the coast. You'll be surprised by the wonderful mix of cultural and natural highlights on offer. This relatively unvisited region boasts hills, barren landscapes, fertile valleys, scorching summers and refreshingly cool beaches on the Alentejo Litoral (the Alentejo's coast). When planning your route, note that some museums and monuments are closed on Mondays, including Mértola's fortress, Beja's regional museum and Évora's municipal museum.

❶–❷

Set off north-northwest from **Vila Real de Santo António**. At first, the IC27 country highway flanks the salt marshes by Castro Marim. Continue along the N122. You'll see increasing numbers of pine trees and olive groves as you near **Mértola**, the first stop on your route (66km/41mi from Vila Real de Santo António). Mértola's medieval castle swings into view as you round a bend. The small town itself sits on a slope leading down to the Rio Guadiana and the Ribeira de Oeiras. Leave your car in the car park on the outskirts of town and climb up the castle hill topped by the Torre de Menagem, its distinctive main tower. It's also worth visiting the luminous white Igreja Matriz along the way. This church was once a mosque, something that becomes immediately apparent when you head inside. The faithful come here to venerate the image of Nossa Senhora de Entre as Vinhas (Our Lady between the Vineyards). Mértola's tourist office is in the Rua da Igreja.

❷–❸

Head northwest from Mértola through the Alentejo's expansive plains towards **Beja** (53km/33mi away). The scenery here is filled with cork oaks. The occasional vineyard and grazing pasture adds a touch of variety to the scene. You'll spot storks' nests up on some of the telephone masts. There are few villages and the traffic is sparse.

As you approach Beja, you'll see the small sea of houses that makes up the town. Just under 25,000 people call Beja their home. Spend the night in the Pousada de São Francisco (Largo D. Nuno Álvares Pereira, tel. 284 313 580; www. pestana.com; €€–€€€), a former Franciscan monastery and regimental headquarters. It's a very good place for dinner – the food is exceptional.

While you're in Beja, visit the crenelated castle, the cathedral and the regional museum that's housed in the Convento de Nossa Senhora da Conceição, a former Clarissan convent. You should also take a stroll over the Praça da República.

Storks nest on a number of buildings and masts in and around Évora

❸–❹

The Alentejo's endless plains accompany you on the drive from Beja to **Évora**, the region's most remarkable city (about 80km/50mi away). The Old Town that's surrounded by walls is a UNESCO World Heritage Site. Check out the **cathedral (Sé)** and the adjoining museum of sacred art. Also visit the remains of the Templo Romano (Roman Temple) and the eerie Capela dos Ossos (Chapel of Bones) that's part of the Igreja de São Francisco. The **Museu de Évora** – an interesting archaeological and art museum – lies not far from the cathedral. The Praça do Giraldo is the city's most beautiful

Walks & Tours

Bright yellow flowerbeds by the Templo Romano, the symbol of Évora

square and a favourite meeting point. It's partially lined with arcades and boasts an 18th-century marble fountain and a few street cafés. The square is the best starting point for exploring the rest of the Old Town, the pedestrian zone and the city's pleasant streets. An eye-catching aqueduct (16th c.) sits outside the city walls.

If you need a place to stay, head about 3km (1.75mi) south of the city to the Monte da Serralheira country estate (tel. 266 741 286; www.monteserralheira.com; €). The apartments accommodate two to four people. Guests can relax by the peaceful pool.

4–5
Leave Évora and drive via Montemor-o-Novo to Alcácer do Sal (a town on the Rio Sado with a fortress and a history of salt production). Then travel along the foothills of the Serra de Grândola to Santiago do Cacém. If you're interested in a spot of culture, make a stop in **Santiago do Cacém** to check out the main church and the ruins of Miróbriga, an ancient Roman town. The castle is imposing, but visitors aren't allowed inside.

5–6
Head 55km (34mi) south of Santiago do Cacém to **Vila Nova de Milfontes**, a true highlight of the coastal Alentejo. This small town by the estuary of the Rio Mira is home to two beaches – Franquia and Farol. You'll find a few restaurants near the pleasant square by the small castle. The fishing harbour is a short way outside town. Travel 10km (6mi) north to discover another beautiful beach, the **Praia do Malhão**. A coastal

Botequim da Mouraria, an eatery in Évora, serves fresh petiscos (Portuguese tapas)

hiking path leads to the shoreline here. Herdade do Freixial (Estrada de S. Luís, tel. 283 998 556; www. herdadedofreixial.com; €€), a beautiful country house hotel, lies around 3km (2mi) from Vila Nova de Milfontes.

6–**7**

From Vila Nova de Milfontes, head south back to **Lagos** (➤ 132) via Aljezur. The journey – a little over 90km (56mi) in length – runs along the Algarve coast.

TAKING A BREAK
Pay a visit to the **Café Arcada** in Évora. It's a traditional meeting point on the Praça do Giraldo.

Lagos is full of life. You'll find some nice accommodation here. It's also home to a marina, some beaches, the Ponta da Piedade's strange rock formations, and the Old Town that's lit up at night. It's a great place to end your tour!

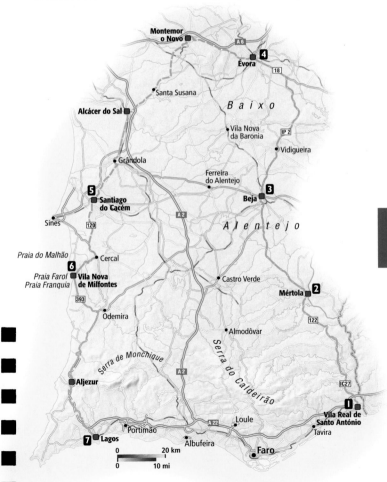

6 IN THE PARQUE NATURAL DA RIA FORMOSA

Walking Tour

LENGTH: 3.8km (2.4mi) **TIME:** at least 1 hour
START/FINISH: The car park at the Centro de Educação Ambiental
➕ 205 D1

This short hike near Olhão is the perfect way to get to know a small, typical part of the Parque Natural da Ria Formosa. The nature park is dominated by wetlands, so you'll have the chance to do a little bit of bird-watching as you walk. With any luck you'll see storks, flamingos and egrets along the way. Don't forget to take binoculars, sun protection and water with you. It's also a good idea to take a picnic for after the hike. You'll find a picnic area at the car park (▶ 187, box). The nature trail isn't very difficult – the path is flat all the way round. 🚻 The route is also a good experience for families with kids.

❶–❷

The trail leads straight out from the car park (**parque de estacionamento**). It's initially indicated by yellow arrows. You'll pass the picnic area (**piquenique**) that's shaded by pine trees on your left. This is where you'll arrive back at the end of your walk. The wide, flat route leads through the inland landscape. The trail soon turns left down an idyllic, slightly narrower path through a small patch of hedges (**sebes**).

❷–❸

As you reach the end of the hedges, you'll see an old draw well (**nora**) to your right.

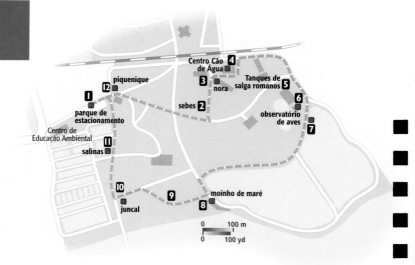

The view from the bird hide you'll find along the route

3–4

Leave the well behind you and follow the path as it bends to the right round the **Centro Cão de Água** (a former dog breeding station). You'll come to a T-junction. Take a right.

4–5

To the right of the path you'll see a cactus thicket, a marshy meadow and the grounds of a bird care and breeding facility. A railway line runs behind the fence on your left. The route now bends to the right. Stay on the broad main trail. Ignore the other paths until you see a sign to some Roman salting tanks **(tanques de salga romanos)** on the right. Dating from the 1st century, you only need to make a tiny detour of around 30m (33yds) to get there. They're flanked at the back by a glittering expanse of lake.

5–6

Head back to the trail. This next stretch is the most beautiful part of the route. There are some great

views of the wetlands. It's now time for a spot of bird-watching. Make use of the first wooden bird hide **(observatório de aves)**. White storks, western swamp hens, moorhens, coots, egrets, herons, common greenshank, various types of duck and gull, and even flamingos can be seen here and on the salt

GETTING TO THE STARTING POINT

Drive 1km (0.6mi) east from the edge of Olhão and you'll find a turn-off to the Centro de Educação Ambiental (Quinta Marim Environmental Education Centre) on the N125. It's not mentioned on the sign, which just says "Ria Formosa". After the junction, drive another 900m (990yds) or so along a side road that runs over train tracks, etc., before arriving at a car park on the left. A booth at the entrance usually provides a small map of the trail and info about the nature park. The Environmental Education Centre isn't part of our tour – the nature path is the main attraction.

Walks & Tours

marshes nearby. Keep an eye out for the Eurasian curlew with its extremely long beak. The birds you'll spot depend on the time of year and how lucky you are. The plant life in the surrounding parkland is also worth a look. You'll spot salt-tolerant plants, marsh plants, pine trees, cacti, gorse, reeds and herbs.

6–7

A second *observatório de aves* lies to the left of the path. It faces the salt marshes. You'll have a clear view over to the village of Armona on the island of the same name in the background.

7–8

The path leads you wonderfully close to the water. The views are simply fantastic. When you reach a fork in the path, turn left to a tide mill **(moinho de maré)** that's driven by the water. It's still in operation today.

8–9

Leaving the tide mill behind you, head inland on the **wooden boardwalk** over the salt marshes (it runs

Black-winged stilts and egrets are in their element at the nature park

TAKING A BREAK
There's nowhere to buy refreshments, but you could make use of the pleasant picnic area near the car park at the end of your walk. Pine trees provide a bit of shade and fill the air with their scent.

parallel to, but slightly away from, the water).

9–10

The boardwalk is joined by a wider path. Turn down it to the left. You'll see an area of reed beds **(juncal)** to your left.

10–11

Turn right at the next T-junction and keep going straight ahead. You're nearing the end of your walk. You'll see some interesting commercial salt basins **(salinas)** on the left-hand side.

11–12

The picnic area **(piquenique)** soon comes into view. The trail has now come full circle. You can enjoy a leisurely picnic here or turn left at the end of the route to get to the car park.

Practicalities

Practicalities

WHAT YOU NEED

		UK	USA	Canada	Australia	Ireland	Netherlands
● Required ○ Suggested ▲ Not required	Some countries require a passport to remain valid for a minimum period (usually at least six months) beyond the date of entry – check beforehand.						
Passport/National Identity Card		●	●	●	●	●	●
Visa (regulations can change – check before booking)		▲	▲	▲	▲	▲	▲
Onward or Return Ticket		▲	▲	▲	▲	▲	▲
Health Inoculations (tetanus and polio)		▲	▲	▲	▲	▲	▲
Health Documentation (► 194, Health)		○	○	○	○	○	○
Travel Insurance		○	○	○	○	○	○
Driving Licence (national) for car hire		●	●	●	●	●	●

WHEN TO GO

High season   Low season

JAN	FEB	MAR	APR	MAY	JUN	JUL	AUG	SEP	OCT	NOV	DEC
15°C	16°C	18°C	20°C	22°C	25°C	28°C	28°C	26°C	22°C	19°C	16°C
59°F	61°F	64°F	68°F	72°F	77°F	82°F	82°F	79°F	72°F	66°F	61°F

☼ Sun   Sunshine and showers   Very wet   Cloud

The table above shows the **maximum daytime temperatures** for each month. If you're not tied to school holidays, come during the best times of the year: in spring (April to June) and in the autumn (September/October). The Algarve can be very hot in summer. It gets extremely dry inland, and you'll find little relief from the heat on the Atlantic coast. The water temperatures at the beaches rise to around 23°C (73°F). It's cooler on the west coast. The Algarve's winters are pleasantly mild, but you won't get by without heating during the chillier months. The beach season extends from March/April to October/November. Hotels (some of which close in winter) are cheaper in the off-season, sometimes cutting their summer prices by well over 50%.

WEBSITES

www.visitalgarve.pt
www.visitportugal.com
www.visitalentejo.pt
www.algarveexpats.com

www.algarveuncovered.com
www.algarvewildlife.com
www.algarvetouristguide.com
www.algarveexperiences.com

www.algarveweb.com
www.portugal-live.net
www.learningportuguese.co.uk

GETTING THERE

By Air: Faro International Airport, the major airport hub in southern Portugal, can be reached on direct flights from a number of European countries. Between spring and autumn, you'll find a great deal of connections from such budget airlines as Ryanair and easyJet and more up-market players like British Airways. There are generally fewer flights to Faro in the winter months. It can be a good idea to book all the parts of your holiday yourself, but you might just find a cheaper deal if you purchase a package holiday from your tour operator. Air fares are at their highest in summer and during the holidays (schools' summer vacations usually last from late June to September in Portugal). Such comparison websites as www.kayak.com and www.skyscanner.net can help you find the flights you want at a price that suits your budget.

By Car: If you're coming from Britain, take a ferry to Bilbao or Santander in northern Spain and drive down to the Algarve (it's around 1,000km/620mi to Faro, for example). Otherwise you'll have to travel down through Europe and cross the Spanish border.

By Rail: Interrailing is still an option (www.interrail.eu), but it can take a long time to get here – e.g. around 28 hours from London to Faro (visit www.seat61.com).

By Bus: It is possible to reach the Algarve by bus (usually via France or Spain), but the journey times can be mammoth. As with driving or taking the train, it's probably not the best option if you don't have very much time for your holiday. If you're interested, check out such websites as www.eurolines.com.

TIME

Portugal is on **Greenwich Mean Time** (GMT) – the same as the UK and one hour behind most of continental Europe. During the summer (end of March until end of October), Portugal runs on GMT plus one hour (GMT+1).

CURRENCY AND FOREIGN EXCHANGE

Portugal is part of the Eurozone.

ATMs: You'll find cash machines in all larger settlements. You can withdraw money with all the usual bank and credit cards. Don't forget your PIN number! Some machines provide instructions in several languages.

Credit Cards: The majority of banks, hotels, mid-/upper-class restaurants, rental car companies, supermarkets and other retail stores generally accept all of the major international credit cards. If you're renting a car, you'll also need to provide a credit card as a guarantee.

Lost and Stolen Cards: Make a note of the emergency number of your bank/credit card provider before you go on holiday. Keep it handy with you in case your card is misplaced or stolen while you're away – your provider will be able to freeze your account and stop any untoward transactions. It's also worth notifying your bank/credit card provider about your trip before you leave, otherwise they may see your transactions abroad as suspicious and block your card.

PORTUGUESE NATIONAL TOURIST OFFICES: www.visitportugal.com

In the UK
11 Belgrave Square, London
SW1X 8PP
☎ +44 845 355 1212

In the US
590 Fifth Avenue, 4th Floor
New York, NY 10036
☎ +1 846 723 0200

In Canada
60 Bloor Street West, Suite 1005
Toronto, Ontario M4W 3B8
☎ +1 416 921 7376

Practicalities

WHEN YOU ARE THERE

NATIONAL HOLIDAYS

1 Jan	New Year
Mar/Apr	Good Friday
25 Apr	Day of the Carnation Revolution
1 May	Labour Day
10 Jun	National Day
8 Dec	Immaculate Conception
21 Aug	Funchal Day
25/26 Dec	Christmas

Most shops are closed on public holidays.

WARNING

Never underestimate the strength of the Atlantic's waves and currents. You should also be wary of the huge differences between low and high tides.

OPENING HOURS

- ○ Shops
- ● Offices
- ● Banks
- ● Main Post Offices
- ● Museums/Monuments
- ● Pharmacies

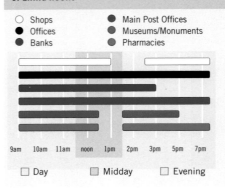

9am 10am 11am noon 1pm 2pm 3pm 5pm 7pm

□ Day   ■ Midday   □ Evening

Shops: often open Mon–Sat, 9am–1pm & 3pm–7pm; **Shopping centres:** often daily 9am–8/9pm
Banks: Mon–Fri, 8:30–3
Post offices: M–F 9–6, Sat 9–noon. Some keep shorter hours/close at lunch.
Museums/Churches: often 9:30/10am–12:30 & 2–5. Most close on Monday.
Pharmacies: 9–12:30 & 2–7. Longer emergency hours.

TIPS/GRATUITIES

Lots of people working in the tourist sector don't have a very good rate of pay. This means they'll be glad of a tip. Only tip for good service, however.

Restaurant	5–10 % of the bill
Bar/Café	round up the amount
Taxi	round up the amount (at most)
Bellhop	€1 per piece of luggage
Maid	€1–€2 per day
City Tour Guides	half day €1–€2, whole day €2–€3
Toilets	small change

ELECTRICITY

 The power supply is 220 volts AC. Sockets take two-pronged round continental plugs. Visitors from the UK will need an adaptor, and visitors from the USA will need a transformer for 100–120 volt devices.

TIME DIFFERENCES

Faro
12 noon

London (GMT)
12 noon

←
New York (EST)
7am

←
Los Angeles (PST)
4am

→
Sydney (AEST)
10pm

STAYING IN TOUCH

Post You can get stamps, etc. for your holiday mail at post offices. Postcards and letters (€0.70/€1.90) take an average of four to five days to reach other parts of Europe. Tariffs rise almost every year. You'll find a postage calculator with current rates at www. ctt.pt. Mail with valuable contents should be sent as a registered delivery *(correio registado)* or with an international courier service.

Public Telephones There are fewer and fewer public phone boxes around nowadays, but you'll still find some here and there. Instead of conventional phone cards, they use a kind of code card that are available from post offices (you'll spot the access code on your receipt). You can also still use coins. Making calls from your hotel can cost a pretty penny.

International Dialling Codes
Dial 00 followed by:

UK	44
USA/Canada	1
Republic of Ireland	353
Australia	61
France	33
Germany	49

Mobile providers and services European mobile/cell phones automatically connect to their partner network when you arrive in the Algarve. Charges depend on your contract. If in doubt, ask your service provider. You could also buy a prepaid SIM card on arrival. Portuguese mobile/cell numbers start with a 9. Non-European visitors should check their phones' compatibility before they arrive.

WiFi and internet Access You'll find high-speed Internet all over the Algarve. WiFi (written "Wi-fi" in Portuguese) is widely available. Whether or not you'll be offered free WiFi at your hotel changes from place to place. The region is still home to some Internet cafés and public Internet terminals (the equipment is usually old).

PERSONAL SAFETY

The Algarve is a pretty safe place to travel overall. Many towns and settlements have their own police station. If you lose your passport, credit card or other valuables (or if they're stolen from you), you'll need to go to the police and report it for insurance purposes.

- Never leave your valuables unattended at the beach or by the pool.
- Be on the lookout for pickpockets at markets, festivals, in and around bars, on trains, on buses and at stations. Keep your bag in front of you and carry your cash close to your body. A traditional money belt can be extremely helpful.
- Never leave your luggage unattended while you're waiting in line to hire a rental car. Also keep an eye on it when it's being loaded onto a bus.
- You should keep the amount of cash you carry with you during the day to a minimum. It's a good idea to leave any spare money or other valuables in your hotel safe, even if they charge you a small extra fee for the privilege.
- Never leave anything inside your car. It's much safer to keep everything locked up and out of sight in the boot/trunk.

POLICE	112
FIRE	112
AMBULANCE	112
EMERGENCY	112

Practicalities

HEALTH

 Insurance Travellers with a European Health Insurance Card (EHIC) are entitled to the same public health services as the Portuguese. Go to your nearest health centre *(centro de saúde)* or to the emergency room *(urgências)* at a hospital *(hospital)* if it's an emergency. Consider buying additional private insurance, but study the fine print.

 Dental services Dental care is run privately in Portugal. Your travel insurance should cover any costs.

 Sun Protection The sun shines all year round in the Algarve. Make sure to protect exposed skin, even when the sky is overcast. The wind is also deceptive – the sun is just as powerful when there's a cool breeze!

 Medication Pharmacies *(farmâcias)* are usually open Mon–Fri 9am–1pm and 2:30pm–7pm and from 9am–12:30pm on Saturdays. You'll find information on emergency and night-time services posted in pharmacy windows. The majority of pharmacists are well trained. If you need a supply of regular medication, make sure to take the leaflets from inside the packets with you.

 Drinking Water It's safe to drink the water from taps/faucets, but it might not taste very good. Buy sparkling *(água com gás)* or non-carbonated *(água sem gás)* mineral water for a more palatable experience.

CONCESSIONS

Young people: Museums often give discounts if you can produce a student card or other personal ID showing your age. Younger kids usually get in free.

Seniors: Travellers over 65 years of age can also get discounts in a number of museums

TRAVELLING WITH A DISABILITY

More and more hotels, etc., now have accessible entrances for wheelchair users. City centres have dedicated parking. Public facilities often provide separate, specially equipped toilets. For more info, visit a local tourist office.

CHILDREN

Portugal deserves its reputation as a child-friendly place. You'll often hear kids playing until late at night. Special attractions for kids are marked out with the logo shown above. Entry prices for water parks, zoos and theme parks are pretty high.

RESTROOMS

You'll find public toilets in shopping centres and at some of the region's larger beaches.

CUSTOMS

Exporting souvenirs that include materials from rare/endangered species is forbidden or subject to authorisation. If you want take tobacco/spirits home, check the limits for your country of residence.

EMBASSIES AND HIGH COMMISSIONS (in Lisbon)

UK	USA	Canada	Ireland	Australia
☎ 213 924 000	☎ 217 273 300	☎ 213 164 600	☎ 213 308 200	☎ 213 101 500

There are two distinctive Portuguese sounds. Firstly, there are vowels written with a *til* (~, like the tilde on a Spanish ñ). These are nasalized, so *pão* ("bread") is pronounced "pow!" with a strong nasal twang, for example. Secondly, "s" and "z" are often pronounced as a slushy "sh" sound: *notas* ("banknotes") is pronounced "not-ersh".

SURVIVAL PHRASES

Yes/No **Sim/Não**
Please **Se faz favor**
Thank you **Obrigado (male speaker)/ obrigada (female speaker)**
You're welcome **De nada/Foi um prazer**
Hello/Goodbye **Olá/Adeus**
Welcome **Bem vindo/a**
Good morning **Bom dia**
Good evening/night **Boa noite**
How are you? **Como está?**
Fine, thank you **Bem, obrigado/a**
Sorry **Perdão**
Excuse me, could you help me?
  Desculpe, podia ajudar-me?
My name is… **Chamo-me…**
Do you speak English? **Fala inglês?**
I don't understand **Não percebo**
I don't speak any Portuguese
  Não falo português

DIRECTIONS AND TRAVELLING

airport **aeroporto**
boat **barco**
bus station **estação de camionetas**
bus/coach **autocarro**
car **automóvel**
church **igreja**
hospital **hospital**
market **mercado**
museum **museu**
square **praça**
street **rua**
taxi rank **praça de táxis**
train **comboio**
ticket **bilhete**
  return **ida e volta**
  single **bilhete de ida**
station **estação**

I'm lost **Perdi-me**
How many kilometres to…?
  Quantos quilómetros faltam ainda para chegar a…?
here/there **aqui/ali**
left/right **à esquerda/à direita**
straight on **em frente**

EMERGENCY!

Help! **Socorro!**
Stop! **Pare!**
Stop that thief! **Apanhe o ladrão!**
Police! **Polícia!**
Fire! **Fogo!**
Leave me alone! **Deixe-me em paz!**
I've lost my purse/wallet **Perdi o meu portamoedas/a minha carteira**
My passport has been stolen
  Roubaram-me o passaporte
Could you call a doctor?
  Podia chamar um médico depressa?

MONEY

bank **banco**
banknote **notas**
cash desk **caixa**
change **troco**
cheque **cheque**
coin **moeda**
credit card **cartão de crédito**
exchange office **cámbios**
exchange rate **cámbio**
foreign **estrangeiro**
mail **correio**
post office **agência do correio**
traveller's cheque **cheque de viagem**
Could you give me some small change?
  Podia dar-me também dinheiro trocado, se faz favor?

NUMBERS

0 **zero**	8 **oito**	16 **dezasseis**	50 **cinquenta**
1 **um**	9 **nove**	17 **dezassete**	60 **sessenta**
2 **dois**	10 **dez**	18 **dezoito**	70 **setenta**
3 **três**	11 **onze**	19 **dezanove**	80 **oitenta**
4 **quatro**	12 **doze**	20 **vinte**	90 **noventa**
5 **cinco**	13 **treze**	21 **vinte e um**	100 **cem**
6 **seis**	14 **catorze**	30 **trinta**	101 **cento e um**
7 **sete**	15 **quinze**	40 **quarenta**	500 **quinhentos**

Useful Words and Phrases

DAYS

Today **Hoje**
Tomorrow **Amanhã**
Yesterday **Ontem**
Tonight **Esta noite**
Last night **Ontem à noite**
In the morning **De manhã**
In the afternoon **De tarde**
Later **Logo/Mais tarde**
This week **Esta semana**
Monday **Segunda-feira**
Tuesday **Terça-feira**
Wednesday **Quarta-feira**
Thursday **Quinta-feira**
Friday **Sexta-feira**
Saturday **Sábado**
Sunday **Domingo**

ACCOMMODATION

Are there any…? **Há…?**
I'd like a room with a view of the sea
   Queria um quarto com vista para o mar
Where's the emergency exit/fire escape?
   Onde fica a saída de emergéncia/escada de salvação?
Does that include breakfast?
   Está incluido o pequeno almoço?
Do you have room service?
   O hotel tem serviço de quarto?
I've made a reservation
   Reservei um lugar
air-conditioning **ar condicionado**
balcony **varanda**
bathroom **casa de banho**
chambermaid **camareira**
hot water **água quente**
hotel **hotel**
key **chave**
lift **elevador**
night **noite**
room **quarto**
room service **serviço de quarto**
shower **duche**
telephone **telefone**
towel **toalha**
water **água**

SHOPPING

Shop **Loja**
Where can I get…? **Em que loja posso arranjar…?**
Could you help me? **Pode atender-me?**
I'm looking for… **Estou a procura de…**
I would like… **Queria…**
I'm just looking **Só estou a ver**

How much? **Quanto custa?**
It's too expensive **Acho demasiado caro**
I'll take this one/these
   Levo este(s)/esta(s)
Bigger **Maior**
Smaller **Mais pequeno**
Open/Closed **Aberto/Fechado**
Have you got a bag? **Tem um saco?**

RESTAURANT

May I book a table, please?
   Posso reservar uma mesa, se faz favor?
A table for two, please
   Uma mesa para duas pessoas, se faz favor
Could we see a menu, please?
   Poderia dar nos a ementa, se faz favor?
Where is the lavatory, please?
   Onde é o banheiro, se faz favor?
What's this? **O que é isto?**
A bottle of… **Uma garrafa de…**
breakfast **pequeno almoço**
lunch **almoço**
dinner **jantar**
bill **conta**
menu **menú/ementa**
dish of the day **prato do dia**
table **mesa**
waiter **empregado/a**

MENU READER

alcohol **alcool**
beer **cerveja**
bread **pão**
cheese **queijo**
coffee with milk **chinesa**
coffee (black) **bica**
fish **peixe**
game **caça**
meat **carne**
milk **leite**
mineral water **água mineral**
   sparkling **con gás**
   still **sem gás**
pepper **pimenta**
potatoes **batatas**
poultry **aves**
salt **sal**
scabbard fish **espada**
shellfish **mariscos**
soups **sopas**
stew **caldeirada**
tea **chá**
vegetables **legumes**
wine **vinho**
   red wine **vinho branco**
   white wine **vinho tinto**

Road Atlas

For chapters: See inside front cover

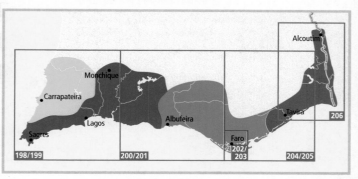

Key to Road Atlas

A 2	Motorway	🏰 ⚔	Castle, fortress; Ruin
	Dual carriageway	⛪ ✝	Church; Ruin
125	Highway	⛪ ✝	Monastery; Ruin
	Main road	🗼	Lighthouse
	Secondary road	🌾	Windmill
	Road under construction/development	🌊 ∩	Waterfall; Cave, grotto
	Unpaved road	⛳	Golf course
	Path, Lane	✈	International airport
	Long-distance hiking trail	✈	Regional airport
	International boundary	★	Point of interest
	Province boundary	🚂	Heritage railway
/////////	National park, National preserve	❈	Lookout point
★	TOP 10	©	Campground
26	Don't Miss	❀	National preserve
22	At Your Leisure	⛵	Yacht harbour
		⚓	Harbour, mooring
		⚓	(Swimming) beach

1 : 250.000

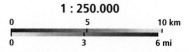

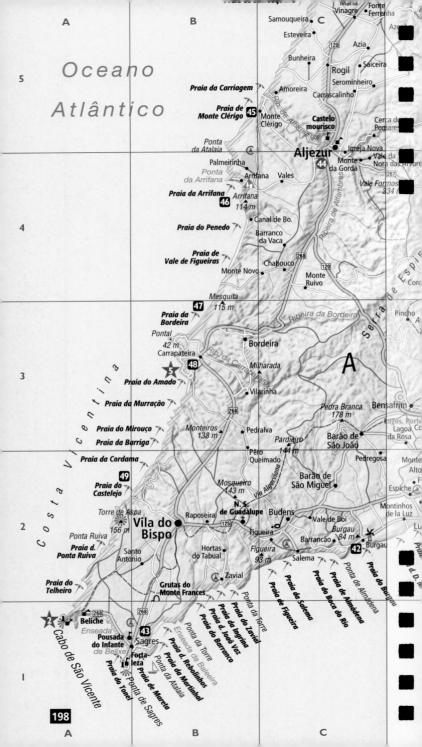

A   **B**   **C**

5

Oceano

Atlântico

Maria Vinagre   Fonte Ferrenha

Samouqueira   Esteveira

120

Azia   Saiceira

Bunheira   Rogil

Praia da Carriagem   Amoreira   Serominheiro   Carrascalinho

Praia de Monte Clérigo **45**   Monte Clérigo   **Castelo mourisco**   Cerca de Pomares

Ponta da Atalaia

Palmeirinha   **Aljezur** **44**   Igreja Nova

Vale da Nora das Arvore

Ponta da Arrifana   Arrifana   Vales   Monte da Gorda

267

Praia da Arrifana **46**   Arrifana 114 m   Vale Formoso 334 m

4

Praia do Penedo   Canal de Bo.

Barranco da Vaca

Praia de Vale de Figueiras   Chabouco   268

Monte Novo   Monte Ruivo   120

Mesquita 115 m   Ribeira da Bordeira

Praia da Bordeira **47**

Serra de Espi

Pincho

Pontal 42 m   **Bordeira**

Carrapateira   Milharada

3

5   **48**   Vilarinha   **A**

Praia do Amado   Pedra Branca 178 m   **Bensafrim**

Praia da Murração   268   Lagos, Porte

Monteiros 138 m   Pedralva   Lagoa Co da Rosa

Praia do Mirouço

Praia da Barriga   *Pardieiro 144 m*   **Barão de São João**

Pêro Queimado   Pedregosa

Praia da Cordama

49   *Mosqueiro 143 m*   **Barão de São Miguel**   Monte Alto

Praia do Castelejo

Torre de Aspa 156 m   Raposeira   **N. de Guadalupe**   **Budens**   Espiche

2

Ponta Ruiva   **Vila do Bispo**   125   Vale de Boi   Montinhos de la Luz

Praia d. Ponta Ruiva   Santo Antonio   Hortas do Tabual   Figueira   Barrancão   *Burgau 84 m* **42**   **Burgau**   Lu

Praia do Telheiro   *Figueira 93 m*   Salema   d. D.

Zavial

Grutas do Monte Frances

Ponta da Torre

268   268

Beliche

Praia do Zavial   *Praia de Figueira*   *Praia de Salema*   *Praia do Boca do Rio*   *Praia de Almadena*   *Praia do Burgau*

1

Enseada Pousada do Infante de Belixe   **43**   Sagres

Forta-leza

Praia da Ingrina   *Praia d. João Vaz*   *Praia do Barranco*   *Praia da Figueira*

Ponta de Almádena

Praia do Tonel   *Praia de Mareta*   *Praia da Martinhal*   *Praia d. Rebolinhos*

Ponta da Torre   *Ponta da Atalaia*   *Enseada da Baleeira*

Cabo de São Vicente   *Ponta de Sagres*

198

A   **B**   **C**

Faro

A

Rua de Loulé

Rua Gomes Freire

Rua Infante Dom Henrique

Rua Conselheiro Sebastião Teles

R. Dr. Miguel Bombarda

Rua da Moagem

Rua Ventura Coelho

Rua Francisco Barreto

Largo da Estação

Estação ferroviária

Portuguese Automobile Club A.C.P

Rua da Barqueta

Avenida da República

Estação rodoviária

Museu Marítimo Ⓜ

Puerto

B

Rua Aboim Ascenção

Rua de S. Sebastião

Igreja de São Sebastião ✝

Rua da Atalaia

Rua da Abegoaria

Rua da Boavista

Rua Teófilo Braga

Rua Serpa Pinto

Rua Baptista Pinto

Rua da Madalena

Largo Madalena

Rua Conselheiro Bivar

Rua de São Pedro

Rua do Prior

Jardim Manuel Bivar

Praça Francisco Gomes

Rua João Dias

Igreja da Misericórdia ✝

Arco da Vila

R. Rasquinho

R. do Município

Centro histórico (Cidade Velha)

Câmara Municipal

Largo da Sé

Sé ✝

Paço Episcopal

R. da Porta

Rua do Tem

Praça Afonso III

Largo do Castelo

Rua Comandante Francisco Manuel

C

Rua F. L. de S. Maria

R. Cunha Matos

Rua do Alportel

Rua General

Largo da Campo da Feira

Igreja do Carmo ✝

Rua do Alportel

Praça Silva P

Largo do Carmo ✉

Rua Cruz dos Mes

Igreja São Pedro ✝

Largo do Poço

Largo de S. Pedro

Rua do Sol

Rua José Estevão

Rua Filipe Alistão

Rua de

Compromisso

Largo do Sol Posto

Rua Lethe

Largo Mo Vel

Praça Ferreira de Almeida

Largo da Mot

Rua Vasco

R. I. de Maio

R. Ivens

R. T. Valadim

Rua Dr. Francisco Gomes

Rua I de Dezembro

Rua de Santo An

Rua Re

Rua da Misericórdia

R. do Albergue

Rua de S. Francis

Rua

Ru

R. José

M. Bandeiro

Arco do Repouso

La

Nossa Senhora da Assu Museu Municipal Ⓜ

Muralha

Rua Nova do Castelo

0   300 m
0   300 yd

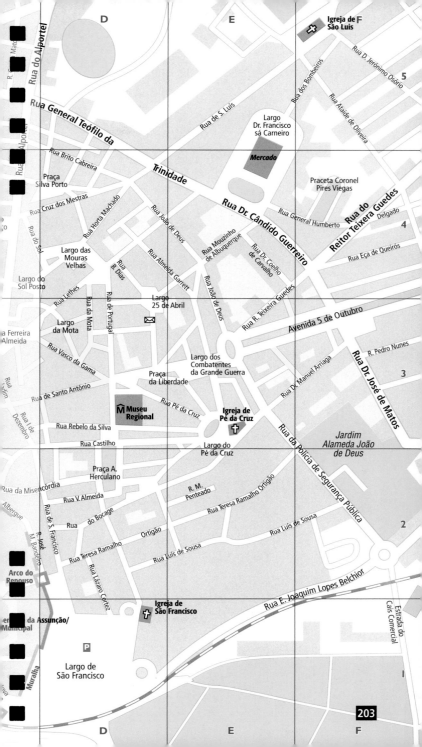

Index

Index

Index / Picture Credits

Picture Credits

Credits

1st Edition 2016

Worldwide Distribution: Marco Polo Travel Publishing Ltd
Pinewood, Chineham Business Park
Crockford Lane, Chineham
Basingstoke, Hampshire RG24 8AL, United Kingdom.
© MAIRDUMONT GmbH & Co. KG, Ostfildern

Authors: Dr. Andreas Drouve
Editor: Petra Sparrer
Translation and revised editing: Jon Andrews, jonandrews.co.uk
Program supervisor: Birgit Borowski
Chief editor: Rainer Eisenschmid

Cartography: © MAIRDUMONT GmbH & Co. KG, Ostfildern
3D-illustrations: jangled nerves, Stuttgart

Printed in China

Despite all of our authors' thorough research, errors can creep in.
The publishers do not accept any liability for this. Whether you
want to praise us, alert us to errors or give us a personal tip –
please don't hesitate to email or post to:

MARCO POLO Travel Publishing Ltd
Pinewood, Chineham Business Park
Crockford Lane, Chineham
Basingstoke, Hampshire RG24 8AL
United Kingdom
Email: sales@marcopolouk.com

FSC
www.fsc.org
MIX
Paper from
responsible sources
FSC® C124385

10 REASONS
TO COME BACK AGAIN

1. The Algarve has a wonderful climate with over **3,000 hours of sun** per year.

2. **The beaches** here are ten a penny, and come in all imaginable shapes and sizes.

3. The region's **vineyards** will produce another great vintage next year – don't miss out!

4. Sculpted by the power of nature, the **Ponta da Piedade** takes your breath away every time.

5. Nowhere else in the world will you see such a fantastic range of beautiful **azulejos**.

6. You'll never get tired of the **Cabo de São Vicente** with its spectacular Atlantic views.

7. There's no major industry in the Algarve, so the **air** is tremendously healthy and sweet.

8. You'll start to miss the region's **people** – relaxed, calm, helpful and generous hosts.

9. The Algarve is an absolute **culinary paradise for fans of fish and seafood.**

10. With hiking, biking, golf and water sports, you're guaranteed a good **workout**!